THE CHICAGO CANON
ON FREE INQUIRY
AND EXPRESSION

the **chicago canon** on free inquiry & expression

EDITED BY

TONY BANOUT

AND

TOM GINSBURG

The University of Chicago Press
Chicago and London

The University of Chicago Press, Chicago 60637
The University of Chicago Press, Ltd., London
© 2024 by The University of Chicago
Published 2024
Printed in the United States of America

33 32 10 30 29 28 27 26 25 24   1 2 3 4 5

ISBN-13: 978-0-226-83780-2 (cloth)
ISBN-13: 978-0-226-83781-9 (e-book)
DOI: https://doi.org/10.7208/chicago/9780226837819.001.0001

Library of Congress Cataloging-in-Publication Data

Names: Banout, Tony, editor. | Ginsburg, Tom, editor.
Title: The Chicago canon on free inquiry and expression /
    edited by Tony Banout and Tom Ginsburg.
Description: Chicago : The University of Chicago Press, 2024. |
    Includes bibliographical references.
Identifiers: LCCN 2024021643 | ISBN 9780226837802 (cloth) |
    ISBN 9780226837819 (ebook)
Subjects: LCSH: University of Chicago. | Intellectual freedom. |
    Freedom of expression. | Academic freedom.
Classification: LCC LC72.3.I3 C55 2024 | DDC 378.1/2130977311—
    dc23/eng/20240619
LC record available at https://lccn.loc.gov/2024021643

♾ This paper meets the requirements of ANSI/NISO Z39.48-1992
(Permanence of Paper).

Contents

Writings and Speeches

Excerpts from Aims of Education Addresses

Committee Reports

Crescat scientia; vita excolatur

Let knowledge grow from more to more; and so be human life
enriched.

Education should not be intended to make people comfortable, it
is meant to make them think. Universities should be expected to
provide the conditions within which hard thought, and therefore
strong disagreement, independent judgment, and the questioning of
stubborn assumptions, can flourish in an environment of the greatest freedom.

HANNA HOLBORN GRAY, *Searching for Utopia*, 2012

The very essence of the life of the mind is the freedom to inquire, to
examine, and to criticize. But that freedom has the same restraints
abroad that it has at home: to state one's position, if impelled by personal conviction, with clarity, reason, and sobriety, always mindful
of the point that the scholar recognizes and tolerates different views
that others may hold and that his view is independent, not official.

JOHN HOPE FRANKLIN, *The American Scholar*, 1968

Today when there is doubt and skepticism concerning the very tradition of intellectual freedom and integrity upon which the intellectual
pursuit of knowledge is based, it is important that the university
through its faculty meet these questions head on.

EDWARD H. LEVI, inauguration convocation address,
November 1968

Preface

Paul Alivisatos

PRESIDENT OF THE UNIVERSITY OF CHICAGO

The Chicago Canon on Free Inquiry and Expression was originally produced in the fall of 2023, to commemorate the establishment of a major new University of Chicago initiative. Building on the University's founding commitment to uninhibited free and full discourse, the Forum for Free Inquiry and Expression brings our long-standing principles to critical action. With its mission to promote the understanding, practice, and advancement of free and open discourse, the Chicago Forum will be a crucible for the most essential aspects that enable knowledge and discovery: the respectful, unabashed, vigorous engagement of diverse ideas.

This volume is a compendium of statements by my predecessors, along with committee reports and faculty speeches, that elucidate the centrality of free expression since the founding of the University, in 1890. Our early leaders articulated what was a truly radical proposition, namely that a new kind of academic institution could be created, and that the right place to do it was Chicago. Far from the established centers of power, Chicago was a forward-looking city that emerged from ashes of the Great Fire with unbound ambitions and unlimited possibility.

William Rainey Harper, its first president, and John D. Rockefeller, its founding benefactor, chose the model of a research university in the Humboldtian tradition, with the idea that it would be a place for individual and community-based efforts to develop mind and culture. A central tenet was that research and teaching should go hand in hand, and thus that the best scholars should be appointed and given wide latitude for inquiry. But they went further. The founding generation embraced the democratic spirit of the times and insisted on broad inclusion in the University community. They were also steadfast in the belief that research was to be undertaken not only for its own sake but for the enrichment of the wider democratic society as well. In this conception, inquiry has a purpose, and the University has a duty to deliver the fruits of that inquiry broadly to the people.

Free expression was the essential ingredient for this alchemical synthesis and has formed the highest principle of the University ever since. The conception of a place for vigorous challenge and engagement, rooted in a telos of ever-deeper inquiry for human flourishing, depends on full expression of ideas. In its role as a place for creating democratic citizens, the University must facilitate student expression. And to have impact, the University requires that the broader culture be open to ideas, even if they seem radical or misguided. Free expression is a principle that grounds not only the creation of knowledge but also the health of the civic community of which the University is a member.

Since ideas of academic freedom and freedom of speech crystallized in the decades after its founding, the University has weathered numerous challenges and has always returned to free expression as its touchstone. What is revealed by this history is that the University is engaged in a complicated relationship with society: it needs at once both autonomy to conduct rigorous inquiry and suppleness to respond to and to be inspired by forces in the world as they reveal new challenges to be addressed. On occasion, the University confronts social and political forces that seek to derail scholarship, which must always be resisted. It is in these moments that leaders have been most articulate in restating our values.

Universities are in constant tension with society, embedded and yet set apart. Maintaining this delicate balance is made possible by only one thing: the centrality of free expression as the cardinal ethos of the university. It reflects a faith in every member of the community, and their ability to make meaningful contributions to understanding. It rests on the belief that ideas are a matter not only of individual genius but of collective conversation, which an academic institution has a duty to nurture. The community refines the contributions of individual scholars, just as their scholarly contributions enrich and thicken the community.

Our own era is one of distinct challenges. The speed at which today's knowledge economies are evolving makes universities more central than ever to the health of societies, and great universities are called on to engage in confronting the greatest challenges that our societies face. Yet the environment for sharing ideas is troubled. We are drowning in a glut of online speech, while virtues of deep listening corrode. Global politics and domestic polarization raise the stakes of discourse. The core function of distinguishing truth and falsehood has become ever more difficult. Around the corner, the possibilities of generative artificial intelligence pose novel challenges.

While the challenges of the day may change, the charge put to University leadership endures: in carrying forth the values and traditions that have animated our institution since its founding, we inculcate in the campus community a shared sense of University-wide citizenship. In this way, it is made clear that our tradition protects the voice of each and every member of our community, inviting all to listen and to engage in a collective dialogue devoted to the pursuit of truth. The sum of this dialogue, noisy and fraught though it may sometimes be, illuminates the gift that is our environment of free expression.

Reading this canon shows that we are in continuity with earlier eras in our willingness to face them. Our collective conversation continues in an unbroken line, traced back from Harper and Hutchins though Levi, Gray, and Zimmer. Each successive era has shown the power and centrality of free expression as key to addressing the challenges that arise, and in each era the University of Chicago has invented new ways of reinvigorating these principles. It is our gift and responsibility to continue this tradition, and this small volume is a tool in that effort.

INTRODUCTION
A Living Tradition

Tony Banout

EXECUTIVE DIRECTOR, THE CHICAGO FORUM

Tom Ginsburg

FACULTY DIRECTOR, THE CHICAGO FORUM

The University of Chicago occupies a distinctive place in higher education, with an international reputation for its strong commitment to free inquiry and expression. This small volume is an attempt to collect, in one publication, the major statements and committee reports that embody and constitute Chicago's tradition of free inquiry and expression. In addition to these official proclamations, we have selected a few presidential and faculty addresses, along with other historical materials that illuminate the tradition's formation and evolution over time. Which brings us to some words of caution and clarification.

We have entitled this book *The Chicago Canon on Free Inquiry and Expression*, well aware that the term "canon" invites critique and debate. Any process of selecting certain texts and not others raises valid questions of inclusion and exclusion. There is also the question of purpose: in its original religious formulation, "canon" refers to a set of texts deemed to be authoritative, and in some cases legally binding. Let us be clear. Our intention is neither to establish a set of comprehensive, definitive texts nor to suggest a sacred or legalistic function. Instead, we offer what we believe to be a meaningful and needed contribution to the ongoing conversation concerning free inquiry and expression at the University of Chicago. We hope that the book is received as a tool to stimulate further discussion, deepening the life of the community as it grapples with the meaning, relevance, and practical implications of historically situated texts.

We use the term "canon" because it suggests a relationship between text and tradition. We assert that the University of Chicago is founded on, has operated through, and continues to extend a *tradition* of free inquiry and expression. That tradition is a multivocal, dynamic, ongoing process. Alasdair MacIntyre's well-known definition of a *living* tradition is most relevant here—a historically extended, socially embodied argument, and an argument precisely in part about the goods that constitute such a tradition.[1] Texts can help in the process of articulating and embodying a living tradition. *The Chicago Canon*, in that way, is an expression of the goods that make up the Chicago tradition—itself an ongoing conversation across generations.

Framing the Chicago tradition as a living conversation about the meaning and application of the University's core tenets invites us to play our respective roles as both heirs and practitioners. A tradition is only alive to the degree to which it animates the life of the academic community, a life that must unfold in contemporary social, academic, and political contexts. We, as a community, both inherit and practice the tradition, and fidelity to it necessitates honest grappling with its principles in the rapidly changing world in which we find ourselves.

A Brief History, in Documents

The University of Chicago was founded by John D. Rockefeller in 1890 and held its first classes in 1892, under the founding presidency of William Rainey Harper. Central to its mission was an emphasis on the flourishing of knowledge such that human life is enriched. This emphasis was inspired by the German model of the research university combined with American pragmatism's commitment to democratic norms.

Both influences informed the institution's foundational commitments to academic freedom and freedom of speech.

In keeping with the German model, free inquiry at the University of Chicago encompassed two distinct freedoms, *lehrfreiheit* and *lernfreiheit*, freedom to teach and freedom to learn. In keeping with American pragmatism, the University integrated a commitment to democratic equality far ahead of its time. This included the open avowal of free speech and, in contrast with its peer institutions, nondiscrimination of applicants on the basis of race or sex. In the widest sense of the term, the University of Chicago was coeducational from the start.[2] The German model's emphasis on free inquiry undertaken by a set of first-rate scholars was fused with the idea of including a wide diversity of individuals within the academic community. Broad participation was a fundamental value, seen as accelerating and enhancing knowledge. Thus, from its founding, the University of Chicago prized the synergy of free inquiry and broad inclusion of diverse views.

Harper propounded a three-part plan for the University of Chicago: the University Proper, i.e., undergraduate and graduate schools; University Publication Work, which would become the University of Chicago Press; and University Extension-Work. The third leg of the stool, Extension-Work, was particularly radical. It went beyond the German research model by incorporating the spirit of democratic pragmatism that would engage the new University with the world beyond its gates. Writing to John D. Rockefeller in characteristically ambitious prose, Harper declared that his plan would do no less than "revolutionize university study in this country."[3] Tellingly, nondiscrimination based on race and sex was not revolutionary enough; University Extension-Work would bring the fruits of knowledge directly to the masses. Harper firmly believed in a vision of the University that "goes to those who cannot come to it."[4] Further, he insisted that University Extension-Work was to be "an organic part of the University," by which he meant integrated right from its founding.[5]

The Board of Trustees adopted Harper's plan in December of 1890, and before the end of the decade, University Extension-Work offered courses at well over fifty locations around the Midwest. It even came to include a partnership with Jane Addams's Hull House, reaching Chicago's exploding lower-class immigrant communities. "The university is of the people, and for the people," Harper proclaimed, echoing Lincoln at Gettysburg.[6]

The flourishing of knowledge, central to the mission of the University, manifests as breakthrough scientific discovery, the creation of new disciplines to engage novel areas of inquiry, and—importantly—the enrichment of human life. Research and impact were integrated, with enrichment the declared purpose of knowledge. The University would distill these ideas into a crisp motto, *Crescat scientia; vita excolatur*, adopted by the Board of Trustees in 1912: "Let knowledge grow from more to more; and so be human life enriched."[7]

Crescat scientia; vita excolatur was emblazoned on the crest, along with a phoenix rising from the ashes. The selection of a nongendered avian emerging from prior ruin was no less imbued with meaning.

> Permit us to assert that at least in poetry the phoenix has for hundreds of years stood for immortality, youth, vigor, and aspiration. Surely this makes it an appropriate charge for the shield of our young Alma Mater. Moreover, no other symbol has been more closely associated with the city of Chicago . . . The rise of Chicago from the ashes of 1871, the springing of our University from the financial ruins of the old one, will immediately occur to all.[8]

Harper's 1905 book, *The Trend in Higher Education*, includes as its first chapter the text of a speech he gave in 1899 as the University of California's Charter Day address: "The University and Democracy." In it, Harper traces the history of Western universities, and identifies their core: "The three birth-marks of a university are, therefore, self-government, freedom from ecclesiastical control, and the right of free utterance. And these certainly give it the right to proclaim itself an institution of the people, an institution born of the democratic spirit."[9] Democracy, in his conception, requires equality and accountability, in contrast with class hierarchy and absolutism. Democracy, in this view, is humanistic. And a functioning democracy requires above all an educated population.

The tone of the speech betrays Harper's leanings as a member of the Baptist clergy, as he clarifies the particular role of the university in advancing democracy. "Democracy has been given a mission to the world, and it is of no uncertain character. I wish to show that the university is the prophet of this democracy and, as well, its priest and its philosopher; that, in other words, the university is the Messiah of the democracy, its to-be-expected deliverer."[10] We elected to include this address in *The Chicago Canon* as a way to illustrate the intrinsic connection that Harper saw between the academy and democracy. From his point of view, history was marching toward greater adoption of the democratic spirit, and it was within the remit of the university to advance that march. While the contours of this relationship and its propriety may be contested—and, viewed from our era, it is hard to argue that democracy is in continual advance—Harper's normative stance remains relevant. Without an educated public, democracy is unsustainable; at the same time, the university needs democracy to fulfill its mission. It has a duty to contribute to public debate through both teaching and research. This address is prime evidence of the commitments to American democracy and pragmatism woven into the University of Chicago's founding ethos.

The late nineteenth and early twentieth centuries were times of great ferment around issues related to labor and capital. The "social question," as it was known in Europe, led to early challenges for the new university. As recounted by College Dean Emeritus John Boyer, the unofficial historian of the University, a young lecturer named Edward Bemis was terminated by Harper in 1894, after complaints from donors and colleagues about his left-wing speeches.[11] Harper insisted that Bemis's political pronouncements were not the cause of his dismissal, but rather his poor teaching. Yet, understandably, the incident led to controversy over the University's commitment to academic freedom. Harper's resounding response came in a speech delivered at the winter convocation in December 1900. Entitled "Freedom of Speech," this document contains many of the fundamental ideas developed in later texts. In it Harper notes that the faculty had adopted a foundational principle of complete freedom of speech on all subjects, which, to quote the official statement Harper includes in his speech, "can neither now nor at any future time be called in question." This jewel is core to the Chicago tradition. It was unanimously adopted in 1899 by the Congregation, an early advisory body created by Harper that included senior faculty, administrators, and alumni representatives. The statement appears in the first paragraph of the University's most recent official report on free expression, the 2015 report of the Committee on Freedom of Expression.[12]

We also include selections from an essay from the same era by John Dewey, the great philosopher of pragmatism, who taught at the University of Chicago from 1894 to 1904.[13] Dewey's essay is of mainly historical interest in light of his role as a theorist of democracy, and also as the founding president of the American Association of University Professors, in 1915. In his essay here, he evinces an overly optimistic view of academic freedom in universities. The expanding spirit of scientific inquiry and the combined forces of public opinion and the press, in his view, would serve to insulate universities from pressure from donors and others. He argued, in essence, that democracy and professional values would protect academic freedom: "The man with money hardly dare directly interfere with freedom of inquiry, even if he wished to; and no respectable university administration would have the courage, even if it were willing, to defy the combined condemnation of other universities and of the general public."[14]

However convincing Harper's and Dewey's arguments about the relation of academic life to democracy may have been to members of the University community, they would not quell external forces from raising challenges. In 1935, Charles R. Walgreen, whose eponymous chain of drugstores survives to this day, announced that he was withdrawing his niece from the University because of "communistic influences." When President Robert Hutchins contested this characterization, the Illinois state senate convened a special investigative committee to explore communistic influences at universities in the state, targeting the University of Chicago in particular. The day after the resolution establishing this legislative committee was adopted, Hutchins followed in the tradition Harper began three decades earlier, giving the impassioned address "What Is a University?" We include it here. Walgreen was apparently convinced by Hutchins's argument; he subsequently made a substantial donation to the University, valued at over $12,000,000 in today's dollars.

After winning back Walgreen and successfully diffusing the pressure of state interference, Hutchins and the University of Chicago would face another wave of scrutiny in the 1940s. Anti-communist hysteria grew to new levels after World War II and the onset of the Cold War. With McCarthyism ascendent and another wave of Red Scare paranoia fueling investigations at the federal level, the Illinois General Assembly once again became a locus of anti-communism investigations. Illinois State Senator Paul W. Broyles chaired a commission in the assembly that sought to uncover seditious activity with an especially broad mandate. The Broyles Commission's wide berth allowed it to pursue "any activities of any person or persons, co-partnership, association, organization or society, or combination thereof which are suspected of being directed toward the overthrow of the Government of the United States or the State of Illinois." Despite the University's deep involvement with the Manhattan Project, the government-led effort that would culminate with the creation of nuclear weapons, it would once again be subject to investigation. Hutchins himself was called before the commission in 1949, giving a concise testimony we include here. Perhaps these two sentences sum it up best: "The policy of repression of ideas cannot work and has never worked. The alternative to it is the long, difficult road of education."

The Broyles affair also compelled University students to protest at the State Capitol, and the ensuing controversy led Laird Bell, chairman of the Board of Trustees, to organize a statement called "Are We Afraid of Freedom?," which is also included here. Bell's statement is unique in this collection, as the sole statement issued by a member of the University's governing Board of Trustees. Three months later, in July 1949, the faculty added its powerful voice to Bell and the trustees. Law professor Edward H. Levi, who would eventually become the University president and later attorney general of the United States, authored a riveting statement for adoption by the Faculty Senate. The senate approved Levi's proposal, included in this volume thanks to historical excavation by Dean Boyer. To the best of our knowledge, this statement has never been published. In the heat of the anti-communist hysteria soon to come to a head in the McCarthy era, the faculty force-fully rejected any (a) stereotyping of individual candidates based on communist sympathies, and (b) the subjection of faculty to loyalty oaths or loyalty investigations. They then went further, calling for the University's appointment of worthy faculty members who have been de-nied or lost their positions elsewhere due to anti-communist sentiment.

We commend a close reading of the faculty statement alongside Bell's "Are We Afraid of Freedom?," as invaluable. Revealed in their juxtaposition are quite different orientations toward the allegations of ideological impropriety. Bell's approach asserts the factual absence of any communist faculty member within the ranks of the University, and the dearth of communist sentiment across the life of the campus. Levi and the faculty, on the other hand, construct a principled rejection of the idea that one's sociopolitical beliefs—as rigid and resistant to reason as they may be—are in any way material to one's scholarly acumen in a separate field of inquiry. The lines of argumentation exhibited here are remarkably distinctive and revealingly emblematic of a living tradition, during a period of ideological hysteria in the country. Then as now, the University's independence was frequently challenged by suspicions of both ideological takeover and excessive donor influence.

On the latter, Hutchins made a remarkable statement near the end of his tenure, responding to a question in a meeting of the Faculty Council: "We always take the position of trying to formulate educational policy, determine standards, and select our staff, then let the public relations chips fall where they may. I am inclined to think the Board of Trustees is hardened to this process, and one of their constant problems, of course, is to influence the community, which is less enlightened than they, to support an institution that stands for the things that this one attempts to stand for. I have no doubt that the position of the University of Chicago over the last fifty years has cost the University money. But whether it has not brought the University money, is another question. It would be difficult to say, financially, whether the University has gained or lost as a result of the positions it has taken on educational policy and academic standards and academic freedom. My belief is that the best way to approach these questions is to approach them from the standpoint of the academic interests of the University, rather than to consider what the public or the Board of Trustees might feel about them. . . . We don't want to change the kind of institution we have because another might be more attractive to people with money."[15]

The 1960s was a time of profound ferment for all American institutions, and the University of Chicago was no exception. During this period, students were active in organizing anti-war protests, and sought to have the University take a more active role in social and political action. President George W. Beadle appointed a committee, chaired by renowned First Amendment scholar Harry Kalven Jr., to make recommendations. Known as the Kalven report, the 1967 document urges a stance it refers to as "neutrality of the university as an institution" with regard to political and social action. Too often misconstrued, the report is perfectly lucid on the intended purpose of institutional neutrality: namely, to cultivate a wide spectrum of views across the academic community. Kalven, as it is eponymously referred to, is fundamentally about the University getting out of the way as an institutional voice, so that the voices of the student body and faculty can more freely engage one another and the world. This follows Harper's 1900 convocation address, which restated the official 1899 unanimous position of the Congregation that the University "does not appear as a disputant on either side upon any public question." Kalven goes further in emphasizing that a robust academic conversation requires the widest possible *diversity* of viewpoints, deploying the term a decade before the US Supreme Court crystallized it into American law as an educational value.[16]

The Kalven report can thus be read as a historical explication of a foundational principle officially articulated nearly seventy years prior.[17] It is an instance of inheritors of the Chicago tradition arguing with themselves about one of the goods that constitute it, the value of institutional neutrality. The argument, of course, continues in the present day. Institutional neutrality has resurfaced as one of the major controversies of the time, with increased pressure from student groups, trustees, and donors on higher education institutions to issue statements on a wide range of political and social matters of concern. In the fall of 2023, Kalven was invoked, debated, and referenced widely as prominent universities faced the question of whether and how to respond to terrorist attacks by Hamas and the outbreak of the Israel-Hamas War. The discussion was framed against the broader trend of issuing institutional statements on matters of arguable relevance to the work of a university.[18] It also highlighted the exceptions that are contemplated by the Kalven report, which are determined by senior administrators.

In 1968, Edward H. Levi took office as the president of the University of Chicago while the nation was reeling in the escalating Vietnam War and the assassinations of Robert F. Kennedy and the Reverend Martin Luther King Jr. This volatile context is the background for two key statements included here as well: Levi's inaugural address in November of that year and a speech he gave one month later, "Unrest and the Universities."

Levi's inaugural address quotes several of his predecessors and is rife with references back to the living Chicago tradition. Restating that the "University's seriousness of purpose was proven from the first by its insistence upon freedom of inquiry and discussion," he also discusses "the propriety of the corporate neutrality of the University on public policy issues." While, as the Kalven report recognizes, the principle of institutional neutrality can be misconstrued as cowardly indifference or insensitivity, Levi's address goes further in asserting "moral aspects" to it. On those aspects, Levi is clear: "Universities are not neutral. They do exist for the propagation of a special point of view; namely, the worthwhileness of the intellectual pursuit of truth—using man's highest powers, struggling against the irrelevancies which corrupt thought, and now standing against the impatience of those who have lost faith in reason." His defense of neutrality on a corporate level did not prevent Levi from describing the Vietnam War as an "outrage." This description highlights how the interpretation of the founding principles always lies with the judgment of the university leaders of the day.

Levi's "Unrest and the Universities" was an address delivered to the Life Insurance Association of America. He begins by treating social

unrest as it pertains to universities as a euphemism for student misconduct within those universities. Despite tendencies to dramatize the
current moment as without precedent, he notes that such misconduct
is nothing new under the sun. Levi points to the "uproarious conduct
of faculty and students," which sometimes led to the closing of renaissance and medieval universities. Levi hearkens back to the wisdom of
Aristotle and Plato on the inevitability of youthful passion and the need
to cultivate respect for the law among the young. Thus, when he turns
to the current moment, Levi has established an ever-present tension
between the urgencies of young college students and the older generations. However, he attends to what he sees as a contemporary problem:
the protest and civil rights movements of his time evolving beyond violations of the law committed with the ultimate aim of legal reform, to
a revolt against law itself. When disruption goes to the extent of cor-
roding the very idea of law, Levi sees a novel danger to universities, because disruptive movements "tend to reject reason which is the way of
education."

In a span of just three years, during a time of great national turmoil,
we have the Kalven report, Levi's inaugural address, and his "Unrest
and the Universities." Reading the three in conversation with one another emphasizes a principled position of institutional neutrality (or
what Levi calls its "moral aspects"), as well as what is at stake should
the university fail to defend reason, evidence, and argument as its
proper modalities. To be sure, as we have seen, the Kalven report does
not merely authorize but obligates the university to act in instances in
which its very mission or core functioning is threatened. Still, Levi's
explication advances the understanding of the ethic of free inquiry
and expression, and the University's duties to defend and advance it.
"Unrest and the Universities" compellingly articulates the threat of
what we might identify as illiberalism in his era, as it manifests in the
repudiation of law itself.

At the heart of the struggle to maintain free and open inquiry in
universities, there is a responsibility to ward off illiberalism. But, in
fairness to the younger generation of students, there were times when
they themselves ably met this responsibility, in a manner that may have

impressed President Levi. In 1974, the University's chapter of Students for a Democratic Society (SDS) took the stage of a lecture hall and began chanting for upward of ninety minutes, disrupting Edward Banfield, a controversial University of Pennsylvania political scientist, who was thereby unable to give his lecture. It was the students rather than the administration who responded to protect norms of open discourse. Student government president Mark C. Brickell introduced a motion at the College Council to discipline the SDS by revoking its recognition as a student organization. It passed decisively, and Joseph Morris, another student government official, drafted a press release. The story was picked up by the Associated Press and made national news, with nearly two dozen mentions in newspapers, from places as diverse as Washington State, Texas, Florida, and Kansas. The episode embodies an ideal in which responsibility for protecting the norms of the community is highly decentralized and all are responsible for maintaining what Paul Alivisatos called the "enormous gifts" of the Chicago tradition.[19]

The collection of committee reports at the end of this volume includes the 1970 report of the University of Chicago Committee on the Criteria of Academic Appointment. Headed by distinguished sociologist Edward Shils, the committee restates the fundamental purpose of universities as "(1) the discovery of important new knowledge; (2) the communication of that knowledge to students and the cultivation in them of the understanding and skills which enable them to engage in the further pursuit of knowledge; and (3) the training of students for entry into professions which require for their practice a systematic body of specialized knowledge." It insists on rigorous standards of merit, without regard to political or religious beliefs and affiliations. In doing so, Shils's committee is faithful to the founding commitment of the University, which recognized openness to all genders and races, based on the individual's potential and proven ability to make excellent scholarly contributions.

We also include a series of committee reports commissioned by President Robert Zimmer, who served from 2006 to 2021. He played a major role in solidifying the Chicago tradition by appointing committees on Protest and Dissent (2014), Freedom of Expression (2014), and

University Discipline for Disruptive Conduct (2017). Each of these included broad faculty representation, and was headed by a distinguished legal scholar, David Strauss, Geoffrey Stone, and Randal Picker, respectively. The 2015 report of the Committee on Freedom of Expression, in particular, has received significant public attention outside the University, and has become known as the definitive statement of "the Chicago Principles." Zimmer's own view of the threats to free expression are well covered in his 2017 speech "Liberal Arts, Free Expression, and the Demosthenes-Feynman Trap," which is included in this collection. Zimmer explicates and defends epistemic humility as one of the core values of a great university as, and then notes how various forces in society are operating to erode academic freedom, a trend that has only accelerated since then.

A revered annual tradition since 1962, the "Aims of Education" address is given by distinguished faculty members to incoming first-year students. These speeches are a rich source of material about the purposes, meanings, and joys of a liberal education. Space, unfortunately, precludes us from displaying more than a fraction of the brilliance displayed therein, but we commend readers to explore the full set.[20] We include excerpts only from four prominent advisors to the Chicago Forum, professors Kimberly Kay Hoang, Gabriel Lear, Geoffrey Stone, and Christopher Wild.

Together, these documents provide a picture of a university that has faced a series of challenges, and tried to maintain a continuous culture since its founding. We can sum up the University's approach in a few core ideas: rigorous open inquiry is essential to the mission of the University, and without it the University is existentially threatened (see the speeches of Harper and Hutchins especially); inquiry requires a wide diversity of views, and an environment of open debate among them; offense is not to be used to shut down ideas; and protest is itself an expressive act that is certainly allowed, but should never disrupt a speaker.

A subtheme of these documents is the importance of norms and culture in sustaining free inquiry. One can see this as early as Harper's 1900 convocation address, in which he speaks of myriad ways in which faculty can fail in their duties. Faculty should not pretend to have expertise they do not possess, for example, and should not insert political views into their lectures. Importantly, he does *not* say that such failures should lead to termination or discipline, for faculty, too, are human. One reason that stating values and principles is important is that it reminds participants in the University community that they have responsibilities as well as rights. Maintaining a culture of free expression requires calling out failures to live up to our ideals, with the hope that we can do better in the future. And it requires self-conscious efforts to construct an environment in which the virtues of free inquiry can thrive.

One challenge has been to give life to the Kalven report's demand that the University cultivate the widest possible diversity of views in the community. As American society has confronted its legacies of social stratification by race, gender, disability, and other forms of difference, the University has had to confront its own shortcomings in integrating diverse populations. While it was an early leader in hiring female faculty, reaching 22.5 percent in 1910, at a time when no peer institution was in the double digits, these numbers declined in subsequent decades.[21] Similar dynamics occurred with the student body, in which women made up more than half the student body in the Junior College in 1902, but saw enrollment decline thereafter.[22] In the early 1980s, confronting a decline in Black enrollment at the same time that overall minority representation was on the rise, the University appointed a Committee on Black Enrollment at the University of Chicago, under the leadership of Professor Dolores G. Norton of the School of Social Service Administration. It recommended numerous steps to reverse the decline. More broadly, despite pursuing nondiscrimination in admissions from its founding (the first African American graduate was Cora B. Jackson, in 1896), actual integration in residential facilities and social life was a struggle for decades.[23] True inclusion is a continuous struggle, not just in terms of race but in many other dimensions.

Another theme that emerges from reading these documents is that each generation faces distinct challenges to inquiry and expression. Our era is no different. Human association and communities are now augmented, formed, and mediated through online activity. Artificial intelligence, though currently nascent, is challenging the place and role of human ingenuity in all kinds of ways. The rise of social media makes communication more instantaneous and renders more porous the boundaries between those in the university community and those outside it. Politics in many countries has become highly polarized, which leads to a kind of tribalism along dogmatic "party lines," from which no dissent can be tolerated. Such an environment is inimical to learning and corrodes the discursive practices that a university environment demands. It thus behooves us to think through how to apply the tradition to a new era, just as prior eras occasioned its contextual reinterpretation.

A related challenge of our era has been the politicization and misuse of the term "free speech" itself. It is thus worth restating what that term refers to in a university context, and in the Chicago tradition as articulated since the nineteenth century. In political life, free speech connotes the ability of anyone to say anything, unconstrained by government. This does not mean that speech has no consequences, only that the *government* can regulate speech for a very limited set of purposes, such as to prevent immediate violence. It is important to note that in a university context, speech is highly constrained at every turn: we evaluate the speech of students to assign grades, faculty are required to stay within the bounds of their subject and possibly their discipline, and disruptive conduct is not allowed. These constraints are critical to maintaining the institution of open inquiry itself, and thus speech here is subordinate to the primary mission of a university, which is discovery and inquiry.

The Chicago Virtues

In his inaugural address as the new president of the University of Chicago, Edward Levi referred to "those virtues which from the beginning and until now have characterized our institution." Taking this historical walk through the major milestones of the Chicago tradition, the reader will note a landscape colored by particular values and virtues. Some of these find explicit articulation, and others are implicit.

Consider the following our attempt to name a set of Chicago virtues, without which the ideals of a thriving intellectual community founded on uninhibited free inquiry and expression simply could not reach its zenith.

Foremost is epistemic humility. We do not know what we do not know, and today's certainties will be tomorrow's punch lines. It is very easy to look back in any field of scholarship to see roads that should not have been taken, and vigorous debates in which intelligent people took what seem now to be quite misguided—even laughable—positions. As scholars and citizens, we should not only expect but welcome the possibility that despite our most diligent and painstaking efforts, we could be wrong. We have been wrong before; we will be wrong again. As Zimmer elegantly argues, reaching back to the wisdom of the ancients in "The Demosthenes-Feynman Trap," it is not just likely but *easy* to deceive oneself. The only cure for confirmation bias is a scholarly community that challenges your assertions and probes your argument. Embrace the challenge.

Each member of the community occupies both sides of that exchange. Our own assertions and claims are subject to critique, and likewise, we seek to be useful to the other members by offering our critique and questions. Even if the affect involved in such exchange is frequently one of discomfort, the challenge and probing is actually generous. Withholding it deprives others of the opportunity to overcome the limitations of their own viewpoint and makes the academic community that much more impoverished. Thus, the corollary virtue of epistemic humility is that of courage. When given the opportunity to interrogate one another, we exercise courage in the generous offering of our genuine thoughts. The fearful instinct to shirk from this must be overcome. The path toward that is practice in the virtue of courage, and this is something that requires active cultivation in an era of social media–induced fear and conformity.

As President George W. Beadle said in his inaugural address, in June 1961: "One cannot search for truth with a closed mind, or without the right to question or doubt at every step. Any injunction to close the mind, to restrict one's beliefs arbitrarily, or to accept on authority without doubt, violates the concept of freedom of the mind." Here freedom does not mean the absence of constraint, but is more of an injunction for continuous inquiry. Implicit is a healthy skepticism of authority. The accumulated wisdom and established truths of a tradition deserve respect, perhaps even deference. Yet tradition alone does not confer veracity, as we respect ideas by challenging them. Such skepticism is itself a virtue.

We ourselves have benefited from conversations within this tradition. One of us still hears the reverberations of the words shared by a wise professor when he was a prospective PhD student at the Divinity School, "There are no sacred cows at the University of Chicago." Skepticism sees no sacrality.

The other one of us absorbed and often repeats a common saying at the Law School, "We are tough on ideas and kind to people."[24] Intellectual toughness need not be tinged with unkindness or disrespect. Assessing ideas and assertions on their own merits, regardless of their source, is the appropriate approach. Thus, intellectual exchange should not personally impugn any conversation partner. We recognize that in our day and age, this admonition is challenging, as ad hominem arguments seem to be gaining in circulation, and are the norm in some social media environments. The virtue called for here is respect for one's counterparts in dialogue. Conversation only works if all parties engage in good faith. Universities must take special steps to inculcate this virtue in an era of online communication. To paraphrase Hobbes, the digital state of nature is quick, telegraphic, and glib, often generating strong emotional reactions that destroy clear thinking if we are not careful.

Who Is This Canon For?

We bring these documents together for multiple audiences. For those concerned with campus free speech, academic freedom, and the role of colleges and universities in civic and cultural life, the collection provides an example of how one institution has wrestled with these issues for over a century. Within the University of Chicago, we hope that the materials can serve the purpose of introducing new members of the University community to its values, as well as provide a resource for those who have been with the University for many years, offering easy access to fundamental texts. We recommend looking at the older materials, beginning with Harper's "Freedom of Speech" and Hutchins's "What Is a University?," to understand the origins and trajectory of the University's approach. For those interested in our current moment, Zimmer's invocation of "The Demosthenes-Feynman Trap" is a suitable and compelling starting place. Wherever one may begin, a clear thematic thread runs through the historical documents, evinced by the frequent reference to preceding statements of forebears. In his presidential inaugural address of 1968, for example, Levi hearkens back to the founding and Harper: "The University's seriousness of purpose was proven from the first by its insistence upon freedom of inquiry and discussion. Intellectual tests for truth made other standards irrelevant. Schools for the propagation of special points of view might exist, Harper wrote, but they could not be called universities."[25] Similarly, the 2015 report of the Committee on Freedom of Expression, chaired by Geoffrey Stone, references many of the earlier texts in building its case for broad and open discourse.

Following the writings and speeches of University leadership, the Aims of Education addresses provide the perspectives of a few notable members of the faculty on free expression. The excerpts included here are all relatively recent. The final section presents various committee reports in chronological order. Some of these, especially those colloquially named for Professors Kalven and Stone, have received a good deal of public attention and endorsement, but the others may also be useful references. As noted above, the Stone report has become synonymous with "the Chicago Principles," some version of which has been adopted by more than a hundred other colleges and universities at this writing.

The longest and densest of the reports is that of Shils and his colleagues. While it is important as an internal reference for members of the University community, it also expresses some core values that may be of broader interest. These include nondiscrimination, the centrality of research excellence, and the creation of a democratic community that minimizes internal hierarchy. For example, it recommends that decisions on appointment and tenure include the views of every member of a department, regardless of rank. This inclusion of the views of junior faculty on senior appointments is not found at every academic institution.

A careful reading of *The Chicago Canon* reveals that the official reports are essentially restatements of the foundational principles set out by the University's founders and earliest leaders. The centrality of scholarly merit, institutional neutrality, and an insistence on uninhibited free inquiry and expression are explicit in the University of Chicago's founding DNA.

It is also our hope that members of other academic communities will read these materials as they construct their own traditions of inquiry and expression. In the spirit of epistemic humility, we invite readers to wrestle with and critique the texts, and do not assert that the Chicago tradition should be universally adopted. Institutions of higher learning have diverse purposes and cultures, and there are no one-size-fits-all solutions. But understanding this set of texts and their meanings, in their historical and political context, can inform how academic institutions wrestle with their complex and ever-changing environments in light of their own core values, virtues, and tradition.

Should such values and virtues not be modeled by academic and administrative leaders of the community, practiced and cultivated by its students, and transmuted by the habits of the Chicago tradition from workshops to seminars and lecture halls to laboratories, the intended purpose of free inquiry and expression could not be fulfilled. Flourishing knowledge, scientific discovery, and artistic efflorescence do enrich human life—that is the bold assertion of the motto of the University of Chicago. These are goods that are produced through individual genius, certainly. But that genius and those goods are refined through the fire of exchange, interplay, and generative friction that only a truly excellent community can provide. It is the structuring and cultivation of a community of inquiry and exchange that is, in some ways, the most challenging work of our time.

Conclusion

Taken as a whole, the robust Chicago tradition constitutes a powerful platform on which the University of Chicago has achieved a reputation for scholarly excellence and vigor. Despite its relatively late founding within the ranks of leading American higher education institutions, this tradition has produced one of the great universities in the world, with a lengthy record of breakthrough discoveries and enriching knowledge in numerous fields. We hope that reflecting on these canonical sources of the University's values will help to ensure that this tradition thrives into the future. Making it so will ultimately be up to the heirs and new practitioners of the Chicago tradition.

Acknowledgments

We are deeply indebted to John Boyer, dean emeritus of the College, who provided invaluable advice as well as several key sources. Tom Miles, dean of the Law School, is responsible for the original idea for this compilation and worked with Ginsburg on an early draft. Thanks for helpful comments to Paul Alivisatos, Hanna Holborn Gray, Gabriel Lear, Richard Shweder, and Geoffrey Stone. We are also grateful to Fred Beuttler for historical references; to Olivia Gross, Alexandra LeBaron, and Elisabeth Snyder for research assistance; and to Megan Gamiz for research. Finally, we are grateful to Elizabeth Branch Dyson, Alan Thomas, Carrie Olivia Adams, and Stephen Twilley at the University of Chicago Press for their input and expert guidance.

writings
and speeches

The University and Democracy

William Rainey Harper

CHARTER DAY ADDRESS, 1899,
AT THE UNIVERSITY OF CALIFORNIA

A Baptist clergyman and Bible scholar, William Rainey Harper was not one to shy from grandiloquence. This address is perhaps the clearest manifestation of the spirit of democracy that animated the University of Chicago's genesis. Harper first traces the global history of the university as an institution, and then declares that democracy has been given a mission in society. In this seemingly divine mission, the university is democracy's priest, philosopher, messiah, and deliverer. His language is explicitly religious, and his vision is of an institution that has a charismatic quality. If nothing else, this address refutes the claim that the University of Chicago was simply and purely a research university in the Humboldtian tradition. Its founding influences also include a strong dose of democratic pragmatism, a progressive-era commitment to social reform, and a quasi-religious sense of mission.

If education and government sustain relationship each to the other, the highest in education must have to do with the highest in government. If national enlightenment contributes to a better and higher national life, the state's chief agent for its proper guidance must be a potent factor in its public life. If humanity, in its slow and tortuous progress toward a higher civilization, counts as its ally a power by which, one by one, the problems of that civilization are resolved, humanity and this allied power must in due time come to have interests and aspirations which bind them irrevocably together. On the one hand, the University is an institution of the government, the guide of the people, and an ally of humanity in its struggle for advancement; and on the other. Democracy is the highest ideal of human achievement, the only possibility of a true national life, the glorious and golden sun lighting up the dark places of all the world.

The word "university" does not suggest the same idea to everyone who hears or speaks it. Sometimes it stands for "college," and rightly so; for the college, like the university (I give the usual dictionary definition), is "an association of men for the purpose of study." Sometimes it means everything. Sometimes nothing. But whatever else it may or may not suggest, we may not overlook the peculiar circumstances in connection with which it had its origin.

The sixth century A. D. witnessed the destruction of the Roman schools, which had represented the older, pagan education. By the twelfth century the church schools, connected with monasteries and cathedrals, and devoted exclusively to ecclesiastical work, had reached their highest stage of development. Three points connected with the origin of the university still continue to characterize it. The earliest history of the first universities shows that they were guilds or associations of men, organized in large measure for self-protection. Here, in fact, was the beginning of that spirit which now pervades every class or trade of men. These associations were "spontaneous confederations," at times of "aliens on a foreign soil," at other times of natives, and in still other cases of the two combined. The rector was chosen by the students, and under his leadership they secured from the community privileges which as individuals they were denied, and they compelled even the professors to be deferential. The university had its birth in the democratic idea; and from the day of its birth this democratic character, except when state or church has interfered, has continued. What, in many instances, has seemed the lawlessness of students and the independence of instructors is to be considered from the point of view of the democratic spirit which gave birth to the university and has characterized every true university. In no other sphere, moreover, did men of different nationalities mingle together more freely.

A second factor was the necessity of securing opportunity for study in lines outside the range of ecclesiastical schools, especially law and medicine, but in large measure also the arts. This is seen in the fact that such instruction was given in the earliest universities; for example, medicine at Salerno in the ninth century; and likewise in the secular and catholic character of the university community, for in the university at Salerno, "at a time when Jews were the object of religious persecution throughout Europe, members of this nationality were to be found, both as teachers and learners." This secular character has at times been overclouded when the church (as in the history of the English universities) or a denomination has seen fit to lay its hand ruthlessly upon the university; but in such cases it always happens that the university ceases to exist, and a church school takes its place. That institution cannot become a university, or remain one, which to any considerable extent is controlled by a power other than that which proceeds from within itself. It is a significant fact that neither church nor state seems at first to have appreciated what was coming, since the first four universities of Italy, after Bologna, rose into existence, like Bologna itself, without a charter from either pope or emperor.

But again, the university had its origin in the desire to make use of new methods of instruction, whereby greater independence of expression and thought might be secured. In the schools of the church there had never been an opportunity to argue; that is, to discuss different opinions. The method had been very simple, to be sure, yet very monotonous. The instructor gave that which he had been given; the pupil received it as it had come down the centuries. This method is still in vogue in some institutions which are under ecclesiastical control. But in the birth period of the university the revival of the study of logic gave rise to the introduction of a new spirit which, although exaggerated and made absurd in some forms of its development, nevertheless freed the work of instruction from the one deadly and deadening method of the past and made possible, in later centuries, the freedom of expression which is today the most distinctive mark of a real university.

The three birth-marks of a university are, therefore, self-government, freedom from ecclesiastical control, and the right of free utterance. And these certainly give it the right to proclaim itself an institution of the people, an institution born of the democratic spirit.

Such being its origin, we may ask ourselves whether it has essentially changed its nature in the development through which ten or more centuries have carried it. The proper restriction of the term must, however, be first applied. What is a university today? I accept, with modification, a common definition: a self-governing association of men for the purpose of study; an institution privileged by the state for the guidance of the people; an agency recognized by the people for resolving the problems of civilization which present themselves in the development of civilization. According to this definition, therefore, only those institutions are universities in which adults are associated (thus excluding elementary and secondary schools, and likewise colleges conducted for the training of boys and girls in various stages of advancement); in which definite and distinct effort is put forth to guide the people in the decision of questions which from time to time confront them, and to furnish leaders in the different callings in whom the people may have full confidence; in which facilities are furnished and encouragement afforded to grapple with the great problems of life and thought, in the worlds of matter and of mind, with the sole purpose of discovering truth, whatever bearing that discovery may have upon other supposed truth. This requires men of the greatest genius, equipment of the highest order, and absolute freedom from interference of any kind, civic or ecclesiastical.

In this connection it is worth while to note Thomas Jefferson's conception of the functions of the University:

(1) To form the statesmen, legislators, and judges, on whom public prosperity and individual happiness are so much to depend;

(2) to expound the principles and structure of government, the laws which regulate the intercourse of nations, those formed principally for our own government, in a sound spirit of legislation, which, banishing all unnecessary restraint on individual action, shall leave us free to do whatever does not violate the equal rights of another;

(3) to harmonize and promote the interests of agriculture, manufactures,

and commerce, and by well-informed views of political economy to give a free scope to the public industry;

(4) to develop the reasoning faculties of our youth, to enlarge their minds, cultivate their morals, and instil into them the principles of virtue and order;

(5) to enlighten them with mathematical and physical sciences, which advance the arts, and administer to the health, the subsistence, and comforts of human life;

(6) and generally to form them to habits of reflection and correct action, rendering them examples of virtue to others, and of happiness within themselves.

The university is naturally the seat of the highest educational work; but again the word "highest" requires definition. It is the highest function of the university to prepare leaders and teachers for every field of activity. It will include, therefore, the work of the college, the secondary school, and the elementary school (with the kindergarten work), if this work is conducted either, on the one hand, as practice work in connection with which teachers may be trained, or, on the other hand, as laboratory work in connection with which effort is being made to work out the solution of important problems, or to secure a more perfect type of work. The sympathies of the true university will be so broad as to bring it into touch with educational problems of every kind.

The university is, further, an integral part of the public-school system. The state, by granting its charter, makes it a public institution, whether it's support comes from the state itself or from private funds. As a public institution, it may not detach itself from the various forms of educational or legislative work conducted under state patronage. Its ideals control the development of all that falls below it. The university, therefore, may not stand aloof; nor may the colleges and schools shut themselves away from its strong and revivifying influence. There may be no organic connection. In most cases such organic connection is unnecessary. The bond is spiritual, and as such stronger than merely formal connection could possibly become.

The university is also an institution of the people. It must, therefore, be "privileged" and, in many instances, supported by the people. In the latter case, it must be influenced by the changes which the people may undergo in their opinions. But the people must remember that when, for any reason, the administration of their institution, or the instruction in any one of its departments, is changed by an influence from without, whenever effort is made to dislodge an officer or a professor because the political sentiment of the majority has undergone a change, at that moment the institution has ceased to be a university; and it cannot again take its place in the rank of universities so long as there continues to exist to any appreciable extent the factor of coercion. The state has no more right than the church to interfere with the search for truth, or with its promulgation when found. The state and church alike may have their own schools and colleges for the training of youthful minds, and for the propagation of special kinds of intelligence; and in these it may choose what special coloring shall be given to the instruction. This is proper, for example, in the military schools of the state, and in the theological schools of the church. But such schools are not universities. They do not represent the people; they do not come out of the people.

The university touches life, every phase of life, at every point. It enters into every field of thought to which the human mind addresses itself. It has no fixed abode far away from man; for it goes to those who cannot come to it. It is shut in behind no lofty battlement; for it has no enemy which it would ward off. Strangely enough, it vanquishes its enemies by inviting them into close association with itself. The university is of the people, and for the people, whether considered individually or collectively.

Democracy means, in general, the supremacy of the people, government for and by those governed, co-operative government. The democracy of Greece, and the democracy of a century ago in our own land, were stages in the evolution which has been taking place from the beginning of man's history on earth. Wherever the industrial spirit has prevailed, as opposed to the predatory, this evolution still continues, and will continue until it includes within its grasp the entire world.

The essential principles in democracy are equality and responsibility to the public will. Opposed to these stand the class system and absolutism. Everywhere and during all time the struggle has gone slowly on; and democracy has surely made her way, and, absorbing from her enemy all that was good, she stands today more firmly and more triumphantly secure than ever before.

Democracy is a government in which the last appeal is to the public will; but the judge to whom the final appeal may be made must be an intelligent and educated judge. The people must be an educated people. Education, indeed, must be the first and foremost policy of democracy. It is the foundation which underlies all else. No advocate of democracy today would accept Rousseau's opinion that the people have in themselves an innate and instinctive wisdom. All will agree with Lord Arthur Russell, that "the multiplicity of ignorance does not give wisdom."

How, then, as a matter of fact, shall a democracy administer itself? By accepting the guidance of those who have been prepared to lead, and by holding them responsible for the trust confided to them. Mr. Gladstone, whose life was devoted to the cause of the Liberal party, once said: "The nation draws a great, perhaps the greatest, part of its light from the minority placed above;" and elsewhere:

The people are of necessity unfit for the rapid, multifarious action of the administrative mind; unfurnished with the ready, elastic, and extended, if superficial, knowledge which the work of government, in this country beyond all others, demands; destitute of that acquaintance with the world, with the minds and tempers of men, with the arts of occasion and opportunity, in fact with the whole doctrine of circumstance, which, lying outside the matter of political plans and propositions, nevertheless frequently determines not the policy alone, but the duty of propounding them. No people of a magnitude to be called a nation has ever, in strictness, governed itself; the utmost which appears to be attainable, under the conditions of human life, is that it should choose its governors, and that it should, on select occasions, bear directly on their action. History shows how rarely even this point has in any considerable manner been attained. It is written in legible characters, and with a pen of iron, on the rock of human destiny, that within the domain of practical politics the people must, in the main, be passive.

And in such a scheme education plays an important part, both with the people and with those to whom they commit the guidance.

Democracy has nothing to do with religion, and yet it has everything; nothing with the specific form in which the religious feeling or religious teaching shall express itself, but everything in making provision for the undisturbed exercise of religious liberty. Where dense ignorance exists, there is no demand for such liberty. It is only where intelligence asserts itself, when education has done its work, that the privilege of religious freedom is demanded. With the church as such, democracy knows no relation; with morality and righteousness in individual and nation, democracy is deeply concerned. Religion itself does not always conduce to morality and righteousness, nor is intelligence in every case a guarantee. But enlightenment of mind and soul, whatever be the single or joint agency that produces it, is the only safeguard against that which is demoralizing and degrading. Education, therefore, in connection with religion, becomes a factor in securing for democracy the very food on which its life depends.

With so much for definition of terms, let me now pass to the question I desire to answer: What relation does the university sustain to democracy? It may be considered either from the point of view of the university or that of the democracy. What part then is the university to play in the great drama of co-operative government? What contribution toward its growth and further evolution may self-government expect to receive from the university?

I trust that I may be pardoned at this point if for a moment I digress. As a student, for many years, of the Old Testament, the thoughts and the forms of thought of the ancient Hebrews have made deep impressions on my mind. In the course of their long-continued history they passed through nearly every form of life, from that of savages to that of highest civilization, and they lived under nearly every form of government, from the patriarchal, through the tribal, the monarchical, and the hierarchical. The history of no other nation furnishes parallels of so varied or so suggestive a character. I beg the privilege of drawing my form of expression from their history; and I do so with the more interest because, to all men who have religious sympathies, whether Jew or Christian, whether Roman Catholic or Protestant, these forms of expression are familiar, and by all they are held sacred.

Democracy has been given a mission to the world, and it is of no uncertain character. I wish to show that the university is the prophet of this democracy and, as well, its priest and its philosopher; that, in other words, the university is the Messiah of the democracy, its to-be-expected deliverer.

The university is the prophet—that is, the spokesman—of democracy. Democracy, if it continue, must include the masses and maintain their sympathy and interest. But as a system it is the product of a long period of evolution, and, as such, is not a simple system. It is, indeed, already somewhat cumbersome and complex. The principles which underlie it need constant and repeated statement by those whose statement will make deep impression. Although intended to be the expression of the popular mind, it is the outcome of movements which have been in operation fifty centuries or more. It is the result of the operation of laws of life which antedate the existence of man himself. Of the history of these movements and of the character of these laws the popular mind is for the most part ignorant. This history must be told over and over again, and the principles made very plain, that all who hear may understand.

But democracy has not yet been unified. Unmistakable traces exist of past ages. The weight of the multitude which it must carry renders progress slow in any case. And without unity the doctrine of equality may not exert its full force. Spokesmen who understand this unity and appreciate its necessity in the economy of democratic progress must proclaim it far and near, until no ear shall have failed to hear the proclamation, no heart shall have failed to heed its clear injunction. The elements which together make this unity must be drawn together and held together by influences that shall outnumber and outweigh those pitted on the other side.

The truth is, democracy has scarcely yet begun to understand itself. It is comparatively so young and untried, and the real experiment has been of so short a duration that it could not be otherwise. Democracy needs teachers who shall say, "Know thyself," messengers who shall bring light to shine upon dark places. There is great danger that the next step, at any time, may be a wrong step. Some such have already been taken; and history shows the terrible cost of being compelled to go back and start anew. Democracy is now able to walk alone, but not infrequently something occurs which leads us to think that there has not yet been time enough to learn how a fair and even balance may at all times be maintained.

Democracy seems to be in the ascendency; but the impartial student of the situation sees many and great fields not yet occupied, while those already occupied are hardly more than nominally possessed. We have democracy in government, to be sure, but if it is a good thing in government, it must be equally good in social relations of various kinds, in art and literature and science. That its influence has been exerted in these fields no one will dispute. But of no one of them may it be said to have taken full possession. And even in the realm of government, how slight comparatively among the nations is the progress of the last century! The occupation of these fields—not by conquest, but by invitation—would greatly strengthen democracy in the places now occupied. Who will persuade the nations to prepare the invitation? Who will induct democracy into these new fields of arts and literature and science? There must be teachers who know democracy and at the same time literature or science, and who, in due time, will bring about the union which promises to the world so much for human welfare.

Democracy has great battles yet to fight. Every step forward is in the face of deadliest opposition. Her enemies are those who sit on thrones and command great armies. Christianity may be democratic, but the church is too frequently hostile to the application of democratic principles. These battles, moreover, must be fought with words, not swords. The pen is far the more effective weapon. There will be many battles; some of them will be long drawn out. The mutterings of war may now be heard in many quarters, but in the end prophetic weapons will win the victory, and "the kings shall shut their mouths, for that which had not been told them shall they see, and that which they had not heard shall they consider" (Isa. 52:15).

Sometimes, too, democracy grows despondent. Borne down by the weight of opposition, overcome by the power of those who for personal ends would see her humbled in the dust, she cries: "My way is hid from the Lord; my judgment is passed over from my God." Discouragement and despair lead to utter demoralization and failure. Under such circumstances, the words of the comforter are needed. Who can measure the density of the darkness and distress which have settled down upon the minds and hearts of the great multitude of men and women in our great cities, for whom, as individuals, there is no hope in life, save perhaps that of bare existence until kindly death shall call them away? Yet these it is who constitute the multitude that is called democracy. "And they look unto the earth and behold distress and darkness, the gloom of anguish, and into thick darkness they are driven away; and they pass through it hardly bestead and hungry; and it comes to pass that, when they are hungry, they fret themselves, and curse their king and their God and turn their faces upward." But now the prophet's voice is heard: "But there shall not always be gloom to her that was in anguish. . . . the people that have walked in darkness shall see a great light." And they shall rejoice; for all oppression shall be removed, and all war shall cease, and a new government shall be established—a government of justice and righteousness which shall endure forever. It is the prophetic voice speaking to a downcast, down-trodden people—a democracy despondent.

At times, furthermore, democracy is corrupt. Under the guise of loyalty to her best interests, those in whose hands she has intrusted herself in loving kindness assault and seduce her. Shame and reproach fall upon her. She must be cleansed and purified before she may again take up her great and glorious work for all the world with a certain hope of success. She has exhibited a fatal weakness; the result will be ruinous. Sharp and stern words must be spoken by the prophet, whose keen eye sees the situation and its dangers. No pity may be extended, no word of sympathy, until the evil has been mended. The lesson is bitter and full of shame; but the effect will be for good, if the chastisement is severe enough. The clear voice of prophetic rebuke must be heard, whenever corruption rears its head to public gaze.

Democracy surely has a mission; and if so, that mission, is in a word, righteousness. It is an interesting fact that all the great religious truths were worked out in the popular mind before they were formulated by the thinkers. The world is waiting for the working out of the doctrine of national righteousness through democracy, and no effort to formulate the doctrine beforehand will avail. But the day is coming when the thought will have become tangible enough to be expressed. The popular mind will not be able to do this service. The prophet, whose discerning eye reads the thought in the heart of democracy itself, expressed in heart-throbs reaching to the very depths of human experience—the prophet, I say, will then formulate the teaching which will make earth indeed a paradise.

The democracy, as an institution, needs interpretation. The past must be interpreted in order that its lessons may be learned, its mistakes avoided. The greatest danger is that there shall be failure to maintain the closest connection with the past. This is necessary for the sake of comparison. Without such comparison we may never know our own position. Every event of past history has contained a message. Every life has been an utterance. These events and lives are to be treated as object-lessons which we are to contemplate, and by contemplation to learn how righteousness may be found. The rise and fall of nations, the growth and decay of institutions, the temporary influences of great characters as interpreted in the light of the present, constitute the basis for all better understanding and all better execution of the democratic idea.

The present itself must be known and interpreted. Its currents and cross-currents, while in large measure the result of forces set in movement far up the stream, must be estimated anew with each fresh dawn of day. The shallows and depths are never the same on two successive days. The charts noting danger signals must be prepared with each turn of the tide of public opinion. And, on the other hand, the slightest turn in the direction of promise is to be encouraged. It is often the smallest variation from the ordinary that proves to be the precursor of greatest reform; for true reform always begins with the thin edge of the wedge. If the present be cared for, the future will take care of itself.

But the future of democracy must be considered. Mounting the watch-tower of observation, the true leader of democracy will make a forecast of the tendencies, in order to encourage his followers by holding up the glory that awaits them, or, by depicting the disaster that is coming, to turn them aside from a policy so soon to prove destructive.

In ancient days, the man who interpreted the past, who measured the present, and who foretold the future was called a prophet. The university, I contend, is this prophet of democracy—the agency established by heaven itself to proclaim the principles of democracy. It is in the university that the best opportunity is afforded to investigate the movements of the past and to present the facts and principles involved before the public. It is the university that, as the center of thought, is to maintain for democracy the unity so essential for its success. The university is the prophetic school out of which come the teachers who are to lead democracy in the true path. It is the university that must guide democracy into the new fields of arts and literature and science. It is the university that fights the battles of democracy, its war-cry being: "Come, let us reason together." It is the university that, in these latter days, goes forth with buoyant spirit to comfort and give help to those who are downcast, taking up its dwelling in the very midst of squalor and distress. It is the university that, with impartial judgment, condemns in democracy the spirit of corruption which now and again lifts up the head, and brings scandal upon democracy's fair name.

The university is the prophet who is to hold high the great ideal of democracy, its mission for righteousness; and by repeated formulation of the ideal, by repeated presentations of its claims, make it possible for the people to realize in tangible form the thought which has come up from their deepest heart. The university, I maintain, is the prophetic interpreter of democracy; the prophet of her past, in all its vicissitudes; the prophet of her present, in all its complexity; the prophet of her future, in all its possibilities.

Among the prophets of olden times, some were mere soothsayers who resorted to the ministrations of music in order to arouse themselves to excited frenzy. Some were dreaming seers, as much awake when sleep settled down upon their eyes as they were asleep to all that was about them in their waking moments. Some were priests whom the prophetic spirit had aroused, but had not wholly subjugated. Some were the greatest souls the world ever knew, whose hearts were touched by the spirit of the living God, whose eyes were open to visions of divine glory, whose arms were steeled by the courage born of close communion with higher powers. It is just so with universities. Some are universities only in name; some, forgetting the circumstances of their birth, may indeed be arrayed against democracy. But the true university, like the true prophet, will be faithful to its antecedents and, therefore, faithful to democracy.

But the university is also the priest of the democracy. But a priest is found only in association with religion. Is democracy a religion? No. Has democracy a religion? Yes; a religion with its god, its altar, and its temple, with its code of ethics and its creed. Its god is mankind, humanity; its altar, home; its temple, country. The one doctrine of democracy's creed is the brotherhood, and consequently the equality of man; its system of ethics is contained in a single word, righteousness.

In this religion there is much of Judaism, and likewise much of Christianity. This was to be expected, for it was Jeremiah of olden time who first preached the idea of individualism, the idea that later became the fundamental thought in the teaching of Jesus Christ, the world's greatest advocate of democracy; while the supplementary idea of solidarity, the corollary of individualism, was first preached by Ezekiel, and likewise later developed into Christianity.

The prophet in history has always been a hero; he has been applauded for his boldness and for his idealistic visions. The priest, on the other hand, has generally been thought a cunning worker, and while his shrewdness has been appreciated, his ambition has been feared and dreaded. In modern times, as in most ancient days, the prophets and the priests have become more and more closely identified in spirit and in work; but the difference is still a marked one.

The religion of democracy is an eclectic religion. It has absorbed many of the best features of various religions and systems of philosophy. It is a broad religion, including a wide variety of belief and practice. It is, nevertheless, a definite religion, representing a clearly defined tendency of expression, both in feeling and in action. It is a world-wide religion; but the world in great part must be changed before its acceptance will be general.

It is the prophet that has to do with creed and ethics, and these have already been considered. The priest is concerned with the religious cultus or practice, and finds his chief occupation in the upbuilding and preservation of the practice. His work is the work of service. He is the mediator between the individual and the ideal, whether abstract or concrete, which constitutes his God. For the god of each individual is that individual's highest conception of man, his ideal man. The priest of democracy's religion is therefore a mediator between man and man; for man is the constituent element in democracy, and humanity is the ideal of all its aspirations.

The service of the priest includes, likewise, the bringing into a close communion, each with the other, of the individual and his God, the cultivation of a deep and lasting communion between the two. This service represents still further the act of consecration, on the part both of the priest and the worshipper—consecration to the highest and holiest conceptions of truth and life. It is the priest who, himself trained in all the mysteries of a religious cultus, himself the custodian of the traditions of the past, inducts those who are of a kindred feeling into those strange mysteries and their inherited treasures.

The university, as priest, is a mediator between man and man; between man and man's own self; between mankind and that ideal inner self of mankind which merits and receives man's adoration. The university, like the priest, leads those who place themselves under its influence, whether they live within or without the university walls, to enter into close communion with their own souls—a communion possible only where opportunity is offered for meditative leisure. The university guild, of all the guilds of workingmen, has been the most successful in securing that leisure for contemplation, consideration of society and of nature, without which mankind can never become acquainted with itself. And for this reason the university is in deep sympathy with every legitimate effort, made by other guilds of workingmen, to secure shorter hours of labor and longer hours for self-improvement. Communion with self, study of self, is, where rightly understood, communion with God and study of God.

The university, furthermore, performs priestly service for democracy in the act of consecration which is involved in her very constitution. And here the old and the modern views of education are combined. The university isolates itself from everything that would tend to draw her from the predetermined service which she has undertaken. Her purpose is a fixed one, and nothing may cause her to swerve from it. She has devoted herself with a consecration received from heaven to the cause of lifting up the folk of her environment—an act of consecration than which none is more holy. But now, though separated thus from all the world for the world's sake, she puts herself in touch with this same "all the world," and no gate or portal fails to greet her entrance. Set apart, and consecrated to the service of every kind of man, she leads those who will follow her to consecrate themselves to the cause of liberty and truth and righteousness, in home, in country, and throughout the world.

The university is the keeper, for the church of the democracy, of holy mysteries, of sacred and significant traditions. These are of such character that if touched by profane hands they would be injured. But the initiated are given free access, and every man who will may receive initiation. No effort is made to exclude; every effort is made rather to include in the list of the initiated the whole world; for the mysteries are such only to those who have not yet been brought to see. Home, country, and humanity—it is for these and with these that this priestly activity is put forth.

This service of mediation, of putting self in close communion with self, of consecration and initiation into sacred mysteries, is performed in the home, the altar of democracy, the most sacred altar known to mankind. The service touches father and mother long before they are father and mother, and reveals the nature of fatherhood and motherhood. It takes the son or daughter, and indirectly touches again the father and mother. Through the school system, the character of which, in spite of itself, the university determines and in a large measure controls (whenever the political machine will permit any good influence to control)—through the school system every family in this entire broad land of ours is brought into touch with the university; for from it proceed the teachers or the teachers' teachers.

The priestly service is likewise performed for and with and in the country as a whole, the great temple of democracy. Enlightenment means pure purpose and holy enthusiasm; these make loyalty to truth, and true loyalty. That religion which blindly accepts what is thrust upon it is not religion, but superstition. That patriotism which knows not what it serves, or for what it is intended, is not patriotism, but ignorant servility. Patriotism, to be a virtue, must be intelligent, must know why it is exercised and for what. Not every man is equal in the work of administering the country's business. Only those who are best can serve best her interests.

Here the priestly service of the university is most necessary, in mediating between party and party; in mingling together as in a crucible the widely diverging ideas; in holding up the standard of consecration to truth and to truth only; in unveiling the history of the past with its strange secrets of successful and unsuccessful experience. Without such work, the service in the temple would be a bewildering discord of unattuned elements out of which no harmonious sound would come to lift the soul to higher and purer thoughts of patriotic feeling.

But greater service yet, if possible, is rendered by the university in that most profound act of worship (in the broadest sense) which man performs when he lifts his thoughts beyond home and country to humanity at large, mankind. As in ordinary religion the great majority perhaps do not transcend the altar, or at all events the temple, their vision being so limited that God himself is forgotten; so home and country, for the most part, exhaust the feelings of most of the adherents of democracy's religion. But the priest, whose great duty it is to enlarge the vision of his followers, takes infinite trouble to teach men that the ties of humanity are not limited to those of home and country, but extend to all the world; for all men are brothers. Humankind is one. And now the university stands as mediator between one country and another far remote. Her service now is to extend to the utmost limits the bond of connection which will enable nation to commune closely with nation. More solemn, sacred, and significant than ever before is the consecration which now includes republics and king-doms and empires. The inner secrets of the soul of humanity (not a single man), of mankind (not a nation) are the subjects of study and of proclamation.

The university is a priest established to act as mediator in the reli-gion of democracy, wherever mediation may be possible; established to lead the souls of men and nations into close communication with the common soul of all humanity; established to stand apart from other institutions, and at the same time to mingle closely with the constituent elements of the people; established to introduce whosoever will into all the mysteries of the past and present, whether solved or still unsolved.

Among the priests of olden times some groveled about in the mire of covetousness and pollution, encouraging men to sin, that they (the priests) might have the sin-offering; some were perfunctory offi-cials with whom the letter of service was all-sufficient; some were true mediators between man and God, and teachers of the holiest truths; some of them in their ministrations of divine things reached so near to God himself as to exhibit in their lives and thoughts the very essence of divinity.

It is just so with the universities. Some are deaf to the cry of suffering humanity; some are exclusive and shut up within themselves; but the true university, the university of the future, is one the motto of which will be: Service for mankind wherever mankind is, whether within scho-lastic walls or without those walls and in the world at large.

Some, perhaps many, will deny that democracy has a religion; but no one will deny that democracy has a philosophy; and the university, I contend, is the philosopher of democracy. The time that remains per-mits only the briefest statement of this proposition.

It was not always possible, in the Old Testament economy, to draw a sharp line between the work of the prophet, the priest, and the philoso-pher or sage. The work of the sage entered into that of both the priest and the prophet; the prophetic ranks were often recruited from those of the priests. But, in spite of some confusion and interchange, there was a marked distinction. The prophet was the idealist; the priest, the formalist; the sage, the humanist. The prophet's thought centered on the nation; the priest's, on the church; the sage's, on the world. From our modern point of view, the prophet might be called the preacher; the priest, the trainer or teacher; the sage, the thinker.

The situation in which democracy finds herself today makes serious demands for severe thinking. By severe thinking I mean the honest and unbiased consideration of all the facts which relate to democracy. Valuable contributions toward the criticism of democracy have been made by De Tocqueville, by Sir Henry Maine, and by Mr. Lecky. But in such cases the vision was greatly restricted and cut short. Only one or two specific statements concerning democracy have been made which still pass unchallenged. The philosophical treatment of the movement has received many important contributions; but, taken altogether, these form but the beginning of the philosophic work which is urgently demanded.

This work lies along three lines. The origin of democracy is still a subject of profound inquiry; and in connection with the questions of origin are those of ancient democracies and their connection with the ancient systems. The history of all this, so far as it includes the main facts, is tolerably well known; but the philosophy of this history is still a subject for investigation. To another division of the work must be assigned the formulation of the laws or principles of democracy. With one or two of these we are fairly familiar; but in detail the work is still the work of the future. That which is immediate and pressing are the special problems of democracy, which have been immediate and pressing throughout its history, and for the solution of which any formulation of laws must wait. These problems concern almost every point for which democracy is supposed to stand. These furnish the work of the day, and with these the philosopher, whoever he may be or whatever he may be, must engage himself. These problems are so old and so constantly before us that they scarcely need mention; and yet the longer their solution is delayed, the more serious becomes their importance.

Socialism, or the extreme and exaggerated form of democracy, threatens to deprive democracy of many of her best friends, and unless checked bids fair to do incalculable injury to the movement for popular government. The rapid increase of the population in the larger cities, and the character of this population, has raised the question whether, in these cases, democracy is able to deal with municipal government, whatever advantages it may have in state and national government. The numbers of the people have greatly increased in a hundred years. Did the democracy of a century ago contemplate that one hundred millions of people were to be governed by themselves? Whatever democracy may do in countries like Switzerland, the problem which presents itself in America, or even in France, is, on account of the vast numbers concerned, something most perplexing.

Within the past three or four decades great wealth has come to a few men here and there, and the relation of this accumulated wealth to democratic institutions and to democratic life has still to be determined. In a monarchy or aristocracy there is a place for men of wealth. How is it in a democracy? Here, too, there must be a place for such; but what shall it be and by what determined? What, too, shall democracy finally determine concerning the great business corporations which, to so great an extent, now control the commercial life of the nation? These are not survivals from an aristocracy. They are the product of democracy. Democracy herself is responsible for them. How will she adjust herself to them and them to herself?

The law-making bodies of democracy are gradually losing strength and prestige. Another quarter of a century of deterioration, another quarter of a century without radical modification of the present plan, will put popular government in a position which will be embarrassing in the extreme. Thus far democracy seems to have found no way of making sure that the strongest men should be placed in control of the country's business. Men confessedly weak, whose private business has been a failure, are too frequently the men who are entrusted with the nation's affairs. Especially has the diplomatic and consular service of democracy (although there are notable exceptions) been weak and unsatisfactory. How shall the strong men be secured for government work? The democracy of a century ago never dreamed that a party machine would be substituted for the will of the people. Is the government of today really a democracy, or is it rather an oligarchy? The problem of the demagogue and the machine is on every side. The difficulty of securing an honest vote is certainly greater than could have been anticipated. Many do not care to vote; many desire to vote too often. In some sections many are not allowed to vote who by the laws of the land are entitled to vote. How shall the vote, the whole vote, and nothing but the vote, be counted?

The church, too, is losing its hold upon the people. For this the democracy is directly or indirectly responsible. The churches are not democratic institutions. The great class of workingmen is hostile to them. And unfortunately the masses make no distinction between the church and Christianity. Democracy has in this matter a great problem staring her in the face.

Education is the basis of all democratic progress. The problems of education are, therefore, the problems of democracy. These are numerous and varied and complex; only the expert can appreciate their gravity. It is maintained by some that in a democracy only the mediocre may be expected in the development of art and literature and science. It is the duty of democracy to meet this proposition; for, if true, it is in itself fatal to democracy's highest claims. The future of democracy is the problem of problems, including, as it does, all others. What will democracy have achieved one hundred—five hundred—years hence? The highest and final test of every plan of government is, as Mr. Godkin has said, its ability to last.

Now, I know full well the tendency of our American republic to sneer at the theorizing of the university; to treat disdainfully all statements which bear the stamp of scholarly spirit; to look askance at everything that seems to bear the air of superiority. But when, against the advice of experience and the plea of theory, urgent steps are taken which soon prove to be wrong steps, how quickly does this same American public turn about and adopt the idea which theory and experience advocated! The examples of this are so numerous and so familiar that I will not stop to recount them.

The university, therefore, is the philosopher of democracy, because it and it alone furnishes the opportunity for the study of these problems. Allow me to repeat the functions of the university as they were formulated by the great apostle of democracy, Thomas Jefferson:

To form the statesmen, legislators, and judges, on whom public property
and individual happiness are so much to depend; to expound the principles and structure of government, the laws which regulate the intercourse
of nations, those formed principally for our own government in a sound
spirit of legislation;. . . . to harmonize and promote the interests of agriculture, manufactures, and commerce, and by well-informed views of
political economy to give free scope to the public industry.

What is this but to solve the problems of democracy?

I have not forgotten that the Old Testament Messiah was expected
to be not only a prophet, a priest, and a sage, but also a king. But the
representation as king was only an adaptation to the monarchy under
which the idea had its birth. When he came, he was no king in any sense
that had been expected. His was a democratic spirit; democracy has no
place for a king. The dream of the Old Testament theocracy was of this
Messiah, the expected one, by whose hand wrong should be set right,
the high ones cast down, the lowly lifted up. And all the while prophets
and priests and sages were living and working and hastening forward
the realization of this magnificent ideal.

Now, let the dream of democracy be likewise of that expected one;
this time an expected agency which, in union with all others, will usher
in the dawn of the day when the universal brotherhood of man will be
understood and accepted by all men. Meanwhile the universities here
and there, in the New World and in the Old; the university men who
occupy high places throughout the earth; the university spirit which,
with every decade, dominates the world more fully, will be doing the
work of the prophet, the priest, and the philosopher of democracy, and
will continue to do that work until it shall be finished, until a purified
and exalted democracy shall have become universal.

Freedom of Speech

William Rainey Harper

A CONVOCATION ADDRESS BY THE PRESIDENT
OF THE UNIVERSITY OF CHICAGO

DECEMBER 18, 1900

Alfred North Whitehead famously characterized the entire history of Western philosophy as a series of footnotes to Plato. What Plato is to Western philosophy, this speech is to the Chicago tradition. It is here that the University's inaugural president succinctly conveys three simple grounding principles officially adopted by the University. Harper opens with these three, synopsizing the bedrock on which the edifice of the living tradition is built. He then goes on to articulate a vision of academic freedom, arguing for the insulation of the faculty from administrative or donor pressure and articulating that freedom's outer limits.

I am moved to make a statement of fact and opinion concerning two related subjects which quite recently have attracted some attention in the public mind. The first of these is the freedom of opinion enjoyed in these days by members of the University. The second is the use and abuse of this right by professors of the University Faculty. Concerning the first, I may be permitted to present a statement adopted unanimously by the members of the Congregation of the University on June 30, 1899:

Resolved,

1. That the principle of complete freedom of speech on all subjects has from the beginning been regarded as fundamental in the University of Chicago, as has been shown both by the attitude of the President and the Board of Trustees and by the actual practice of the President and the professors.

2. That this principle can neither now nor at any future time be called in question.

3. That it is desirable to have it clearly understood that the University, as such, does not appear as a disputant on either side upon any public question; and that the utterances which any professor may make in public are to be regarded as representing his own opinions only.

To this statement of the Congregation I wish to add, first, that whatever may or may not have happened in other universities, in the University of Chicago neither the Trustees, nor the President, nor anyone in official position has at any time called an instructor to account for any public utterances which he may have made. Still further, in no single case has a donor of the University called the attention of the Trustees to the teaching of any officer of the University as being distasteful or objectionable. Still further, it is my opinion that no donor of money to a University, whether that donor be an individual or the state, has any right, before God or man, to interfere with the teaching of officers appointed to give instruction in a university. When for any reason, in a university on private foundation or in a university supported by public money, the administration of the institution or the instruction in any one of its departments is changed by an influence from without; when an effort is made to dislodge an officer or a professor because the political sentiment or the religious sentiment of the majority has undergone a change, at that moment the institution has ceased to be a university, and it cannot again take its place in the rank of universities so long as there continues to exist to any appreciable extent the factor of coercion. Neither an individual, nor the state, nor the church has the right to interfere with the search for truth, or with its promulgation when found. Individuals or the state or the church may found schools for propagating certain special kinds of instruction, but such schools are not universities, and may not be so denominated. A donor has the privilege of ceasing to make his gifts to an institution if, in his opinion, for any reason, the work of the institution is not satisfactory; but *as donor* he has no right to interfere with the administration of the instruction of the university. The trustees in an institution in which such interference has taken place may not maintain their self-respect and remain trustees. They owe it to themselves and to the cause of liberty of thought to resign their places rather than to yield a principle the significance of which rises above all else in comparison. In order to be specific, and in order not to be misunderstood, I wish to say again that no donor of funds to the University, and I include in the number of donors the founder of the University, Mr. Rockefeller, has ever by a single word or act indicated his dissatisfaction with the instruction given to students in the University, or with the public expression of opinion made by an officer of the University. I vouch for the truth of this statement, and I trust that it may have the largest possible publicity.

Concerning the second subject, the use and abuse of the right of free expression by officers of the University staff. As I have said, an instructor in the University has an absolute right to express his opinion. If such an instructor is on an appointment for two or three or four years, and if during these years he exercises this right in such a way as to do himself and the institution serious injury, it is of course the privilege of the University to allow his appointment to lapse at the end of the term for which it was originally made. If an officer on permanent appointment abuses his privilege as a professor, the University must suffer and it is proper that it should suffer. This is only the direct and inevitable consequence of the lack of foresight and wisdom involved in the original appointment. The injury thus accruing to the University is moreover far less serious than would follow, if, for an expression of opinion differing from that of the majority of the Faculty or from that of the Board of Trustees or from that of the President of the University, a permanent officer might be asked to present his resignation. The greatest single element necessary for the cultivation of the academic spirit is the feeling of security from interference. It is only those who have this feeling that are able to do work which in the highest sense will be beneficial to humanity. Freedom of expression must be given the members of a university faculty even though it be abused, for, as has been said, the abuse of it is not so great an evil as the restriction of such liberty. But it may be asked, in what way may the professor abuse his privilege of freedom of expression? or to put the question more largely, in what way does a professor bring reproach and injury to himself and to his institution? I answer, a professor is guilty of an abuse of his privilege who promulgates as truth ideas or opinions which have not been tested scientifically by his colleagues in the same department of research or investigation. A professor has no right to proclaim to the public as truth discovered that which is yet unsettled and uncertain. A professor abuses his privilege who takes advantage of a class-room exercise to propagate the partisan views of one or another of the political parties. The university is no place for partisanship. From the teacher's desk should emanate the discussion of principles, the judicial statements of arguments from various points of view, and not the one-sided representations of a partisan character. A professor abuses his privilege who in any way seeks to influence his pupils or the public by sensational methods. A professor abuses his privilege of expression of opinion when although a student and perhaps an authority in one department or group of departments he undertakes to speak authoritatively on subjects which have no relationship to the department in which he was appointed to give instruction. A professor abuses his privilege in many cases when, although shut off in large measure from the world, and engaged within a narrow field of investigation, he undertakes to instruct his colleagues or the public concerning matters in the world at large in connection with which he has had little or no experience. A professor abuses his privilege of freedom of expression of opinion when he fails to exercise that quality, which it must be confessed in some cases the professor lacks, ordinarily called common sense. A professor ought not to make such an exhibition of his weakness or to make an exhibition of his weakness so many times that the attention of the public at large is called to the fact. In this respect he has no larger liberty than other men.

But may a professor do all of these things and yet remain an officer in the University? Yes. The professor in most cases is only an ordinary man. Perfection is not to be expected of him. Like men in other professions, professors have their weaknesses. But will a professor under any circumstances be asked to withdraw from the University? Yes. His resignation will be demanded and will be accepted, when, in the opinion of those in authority, he has been guilty of immorality, or when for any reason he has proved himself to be incompetent to perform the service called for. The public should be on its guard in two particulars: the utterance of a professor, however wise or foolish, is not the utterance of the University. No individual, no group of individuals can speak for the University. A statement, by whomsoever made, is the statement of an individual.

And further, in passing judgment, care should be taken that the facts are known. It is a habit of modern journalists, and especially of the average student reporter for the newspapers, so to supply facts, so to dress up the real facts, so to magnify and exaggerate, so to belittle and ridicule universities and university men, that serious injury is wrought, where perhaps no such injury was intended. It is the fashion to do this sort of thing, and it is done regardless of the consequences. Real regard for the interests of higher education would lead to the adoption of a different policy; but, as matters stand, the professor is often charged with an imbecility which is not characteristic of him, and to him there are frequently ascribed startling and revolutionary sentiments and statements of which he is wholly innocent. I may sum up the point in three sentences: (1) college and university professors do make mistakes and sometimes serious ones; but (2) these are to be attributed to the professor, not to the university; and (3) in a large majority of instances the mistake, as published to the world, is misrepresented, exaggerated, or, at least, presented in such a form as to do the professor, the university, and the cause of truth itself, gross injustice.

Academic Freedom

John Dewey

EDUCATIONAL REVIEW

JANUARY–MAY 1902

For a decade of his career, the preeminent philosopher of American pragmatism made the University of Chicago his academic home. Joining the faculty as chair of the Department of Philosophy in 1894, John Dewey did some of his foundational work on education at Chicago. His commitment to active participation in the formation of values critical to the practice of democracy led him to establish the University's Laboratory School, which continues to serve students from the lower grades through high school. In this essay, Dewey propounds on academic freedom more than a decade before he helped to found the American Association of University Professors, whose 1915 "Declaration of Principles on Academic Freedom and Tenure" remains one of the most important documents defining the meaning of academic freedom. Dewey left Chicago in 1904 in a dispute over the Laboratory School.

In discussing the questions summed up in the phrase academic freedom, it is necessary to make a distinction between the university proper and those teaching bodies, called by whatever name, whose primary business is to inculcate a fixed set of ideas and facts. The former aims to discover and communicate truth and to make its recipients better judges of truth and more effective in applying it to the affairs of life. The latter have as their aim the perpetuation of a certain way of looking at things current among a given body of persons. Their purpose is to disciple rather than to discipline—not indeed at the expense of truth, but in such a way as to conserve what is already regarded as truth by some considerable body of persons. The problem of freedom of inquiry and instruction clearly assumes different forms in these two types of institutions. An ecclesiastical, political, or even economic corporation holding certain tenets certainly has a right to support an institution to maintain and propagate its creed. It is a question not so much of freedom of thought as of ability to secure competent teachers willing to work under such conditions, to pay bills, and to have a constituency from which to draw students. Needless to say, the line between these two types of institutions is not so clear-cut in practice as it is in theory. Many institutions are in a state of transition. Historically, they are bound by ties to some particular body of beliefs, generally to some denominational association. Nominally, they still owe a certain allegiance to a particular body. But they are also assuming many strictly university functions and are thereby accepting obligations to a larger world of scholarship and of society. In these respects the institution imposes upon its teaching corps not merely a right, but a duty, to maintain in all ways the university ideal of freedom of inquiry and freedom of communication. But, in other respects, while the historical denominational ties are elongated and attenuated, they still remain; and thru them the instructor is to some extent bound. Implicit, if not explicit, obligations are assumed. In this situation, conflict between the two concerns of the university may arise; and in the confusion of this conflict it is difficult to determine just which way the instructor is morally bound to face. Upon the whole it is clear, however, that the burden falls upon the individual. If he finds that the particular and local attachment is so strong as to limit him in the pursuit of what he regards as essential, there is one liberty which cannot be taken away from him: the liberty of finding a more congenial sphere of work. So far as the institution is frank in acknowledging and maintaining its denominational connections, he cannot throw the burden back upon it. Nevertheless he, and those who are like-minded, have the right to deplore what they consider as a restriction, and to hope and labor for the time when the obligation in behalf of all the truth to society at large shall be felt as more urgent than that of a part of truth to a part of society.

But it cannot be inferred that the problem is a wholly simple one, even within the frankly announced denominational institutions. The line in almost any case is a shifting one. I am told that a certain denominational college permits and encourages a good deal of instruction in anatomy and physiology because there is biblical authority for the statement that the human body is fearfully and wonderfully made, while it looks askance upon the teaching of geology because the recognized doctrine of the latter appears to it to conflict with the plain statements of Genesis. As regards anatomy and physiology, an instructor in such an institution would naturally feel that his indebtedness was to the world of scholarship rather than to his own denomination, and here conflict might possibly arise. Or a teacher of history might find a conflict existing between the supposed interests of his denomination and the historical facts as determined by the best research at his command. Here, again, he would find himself naturally pulled in two different directions. No possible tie to what his own institution specially stands for can impose upon him the obligation to suppress the truth as he sees it. I quote such cases simply to indicate that, while in a general way there is a line of demarcation between the two types of institutions referred to, and consequently the problem of academic freedom does not arise so definitely in one type, yet even in the latter, because all things shift, the question, after all, may assert itself.

In the subsequent discussion I shall confine myself exclusively to institutions of the university type. It is clear that in this sphere any attack, or even any restriction, upon academic freedom is directed against the university itself. To investigate truth; critically to verify fact; to reach conclusions by means of the best methods at command, untrammeled by external fear or favor, to communicate this truth to the student; to interpret to him its bearing on the questions he will have to face in life— this is precisely the aim and object of the university. To aim a blow at any one of these operations is to deal a vital wound to the university itself. The university function is the truth-function. At one time it may be more concerned with the tradition or transmission of truth, and at another time with its discovery. Both functions are necessary, and neither can ever be entirely absent. The exact ratio between them depends upon local and temporal considerations rather than upon anything inherent in the university. The one thing that is inherent and essential is the idea of truth.

So clear are these principles that, in the abstract, no theoretical problem can possibly arise. The difficulties arise from two concrete sources. In the first place, there is no gainsaying the fact that some of the studies taught in the university are inherently in a much more scientific condition than others. In the second place, the popular or general recognition of scientific status is much more widespread as regards some subjects than others. Upon the whole, it is practically impossible for any serious question regarding academic freedom to arise in the sphere of mathematics, astronomy, physics, or chemistry. Each of these subjects has now its definite established technique, and its own sphere within which it is supreme. This is so as fact; and it is generally so recognized by all persons of influence in the community. Consequently, there is no leverage from which to direct an attack upon academic freedom in any of these subjects. Such, of course, was not the case a few centuries ago. We know the storm that raged about astronomy. We know that it is only thru great trial and tribulation that the sciences have worked out such a definite body of truth and such definite instrumentalities of inquiry and verification as to give them a position assured from attack.

The biological sciences are clearly in a transitional state. The conception of evolution is a test case. It is safe to say that no university worthy of the name would put any limitation upon instruction in this theory, or upon its use as an agency of research and classification. Very little sympathy could be secured for an attack upon a university for encouraging the use of this theory. Many of the smaller colleges, however, would be shaken to their foundations by anything that seemed like a public avowal of belief in this doctrine. These facts would seem to mean that the more influential sections of the community upon which the universities properly depend have adjusted themselves to the fact that biology is a science which must be the judge of its own methods of work; that its facts and tests of fact are to be sought within its own scientific operations, and not in any extraneous sources. There are still, however, large portions of society which have not come to recognize that biology is an established science, and which, therefore, cannot concede to it the right to determine belief in regions that conflict with received opinions, and with the emotions that cluster about them.

There is another group of sciences which, from the standpoint of definitive method and a clearly accepted body of verified fact, are more remote from a scientific status. I refer especially to the social and psychological disciplines, and to some phases of linguistic and historical study—those most intimately associated with religious history and literature. Moreover, the public recognition of the scientific status attained lags behind the fact. As compared with mathematics or physics we can employ the term "science" only in a tentative and somewhat prophetic sense—the aspirations, the tendencies, the movement are scientific. But to the public at large the facts and relations with which these topics deal are still almost wholly in the region of opinion, prejudice, and accepted tradition. It has hardly dawned upon the community as a whole that science really has anything to say upon matters in the social and psychological sphere. The general public may be willing enough to admit in the abstract the existence of a science of political economy, sociology, or psychology, but when these dare to emerge from a remote and technical sphere, and pass authoritative judgment upon affairs of daily life,—when they come in contact, that is, with the interests of daily life,—they meet with little but skepticism or hostility or, what is worse, sensational exploitation.

It is out of these two facts—the backwardness of some of our sciences and failure of the general public to recognize even the amount of advance actually made—that the concrete problems of academic freedom arise. The case may be stated as follows: On behalf of academic freedom it may be urged that the only way in which the more backward subjects can possibly reach anything like the status of mathematics and mechanics is by encouraging to the utmost freedom of investigation, and the publication, oral and printed, of the results of inquiry. It may be urged that the very failure on the part of the public to recognize rightful jurisdiction for scientific methods and results is only the more reason for unusual frankness and fullness of expression. Because the public is so behind the scientific times, it must be brought up. The points of contact, it may be urged, between the social and moral sciences and social needs, are even more numerous and more urgent than in the case of the mathematical and physical sciences. The latter have secured their independence thru a certain abstractness, a certain remoteness from matters of social concern. Political economy, sociology, historical interpretation, psychology in its various possible applications, deal face to face with problems of life, not with problems of technical theory. Hence the right and duty of academic freedom are even greater here than elsewhere.

Per contra, it may be pointed out that, in so far as these subjects have not reached a scientific status, an expression of opinion on the part of a university instructor remains after all nothing but an expression of opinion, and hardly entitled to any more weight than that of any other reasonably intelligent person. It, however, is almost certain to be regarded as an official judgment. It thus commits and possibly compromises the institution to which the instructor belongs. The sphere of ideas which has not yet come under recognized scientific control is, moreover, precisely that which is bound up most closely with deep-rooted prejudice and intense emotional reaction. These, in turn, exist because of habits and modes of life to which the people have accustomed themselves. To attack them is to appear to be hostile to institutions with which the worth of life is bound up.

John Stuart Mill, with characteristic insight, somewhere points out that the German easily tolerates and welcomes all kinds of new ideas and new speculations because they exist in a region apart; they do not affect, excepting indirectly, the practical conduct of life. With the Englishman it is different. He is instinctively uneasy in the presence of a new idea; the wider the scope of the idea, the more readily uneasiness turns to suspicion and hostility. He recognizes that to accept the new idea means a change in the institutions of life. The idea is too serious a matter to be trifled with. The American has certainly inherited enough of the Englishman's sense for the connection of theory and practice to be conservative in the matter of the public broaching (and under modern conditions even classroom discussion is quasi-public) of ideas which lie much beyond the bounds of the domain publicly allotted to science.

Wherever scientific method is only partially attained the danger of undue dogmatism and of partisanship is very great. It is possible to consecrate ideas born of sheer partisanship with the halo of scientifically established belief. It is possible to state what is currently recognized to be scientific truth in such a way as to violate the most sacred beliefs of a large number of our fellow-men. The manner of conveying the truth may cause an irritation quite foreign to its own substance. This is quite likely to be the case whenever the negative rather than the positive aspect is dwelt upon; wherever the discrepancy between the new truth and established institutions is emphasized, rather than the intrinsic significance of the new conception. The outcome is disintegrating instead of constructive; and the methods inevitably breed distrust and antagonism.

One might, for example, be scientifically convinced of the transitional character of the existing capitalistic control of industrial affairs and its reflected influences upon political life; one might be convinced that many and grave evils and injustices are incident to it, and yet never raise the question of academic freedom, although developing his views with definiteness and explicitness. He might go at the problem in such an objective, historic, and constructive manner as not to excite the prejudices or inflame the passions even of those who thoroughly disagreed with him. On the other hand, views at the bottom exactly the same can be stated in such a way as to rasp the feelings of everyone exercising the capitalistic function. What will stand or fall upon its own scientific merits, if presented as a case of objective social evolution, is mixed up with all sorts of extraneous and passion-inflaming factors when set forth as the outcome of the conscious and aggressive selfishness of a class.

As a result of such influences the problem of academic freedom becomes to a very large extent a personal matter. I mean that it is a matter of the scholarship, judgment, and sympathy of the individual in dealing with matters either only just coming within the range of strict scientific treatment, or, even if fairly annexed to the scientific domain, not yet recognized by contemporary public opinion as belonging there. All sorts of difficulties arise when we attempt to lay down any rules for, or pass any judgment upon, the personal aspects of the matter. Such rules are likely to be innocuous truisms. We can insist upon one hand that the individual must be loyal to truth, and that he must have the courage of his convictions; that he must not permit their presumed unpopularity, the possibly unfavorable reaction of their free expression upon his own career, to swerve him from his singleness of devotion to truth. We may dwell upon the dangers of moral cowardice and of turning traitor to the cause in which every scholar is enlisted. We may indicate the necessity of the use of common sense in the expression of views on controverted points, especially points entering into the arena of current religious and political discussion. We may insist that a man needs tact as well as scholarship; or, let us say, sympathy with human interests—since "tac" suggests perhaps too much a kind of juggling diplomacy with the questions at issue.

It is possible to confuse loyalty to truth with self-conceit in the assertion of personal opinion. It is possible to identify courage with bumptiousness. Lack of reverence for the things that mean much to humanity, joined with a craving for public notoriety, may induce a man to pose as a martyr to truth when in reality he is a victim of his own lack of mental and moral poise. President Harper, in a clear and comprehensive discussion in his Convocation Address of December, 1900,[1] points out so clearly the sources of personal failure of this sort that I make no apology for quoting his words:

(1) A professor is guilty of an abuse of privilege who promulgates as truth ideas or opinions which have not been tested scientifically by his colleagues in the same department of research or investigation. (2) A professor abuses his privilege who takes advantage of a classroom exercise to propagate the partisan view of one or another of the political parties. (3) A professor abuses his privilege who in any way seeks to influence his pupils or the public by sensational methods. (4) A professor abuses his privilege of expression of opinion when, although a student and perhaps an authority in one department or group of departments,

he undertakes to speak authoritatively on subjects which have no relationship to the department in which he was appointed to give instruction. (5) A professor abuses his privilege in many cases when, although shut off in large measure from the world and engaged within a narrow field of investigation, he undertakes to instruct his colleagues or the public concerning matters in the world at large in connection with which he has had little or no experience.

Now, while all university men will doubtless agree with President Harper when he says "freedom of expression must be given to members of a university faculty, even though it be abused, for the abuse of it is not so great an evil as the restriction of such liberty," yet it is clear that the presence of these personal elements detracts very much from the simplicity and significance of an issue regarding academic freedom. For reasons into which I cannot fully go, I am convinced that it is now well-nigh impossible to have raised, in any of the true universities of this country, a straight out-and-out issue of academic freedom. The constantly increasing momentum of scientific inquiry, the increasing sense of the university spirit binding together into one whole the scattered members of various faculties throughout the country, the increased sensitiveness of public opinion, and the active willingness of a large part of the public press to seize upon and even to exaggerate anything squinting towards an infringement upon the rights of free inquiry and free speech—these reasons, among others, make me dissent most thoroughly from the opinion sometimes expressed that there is a growing danger threatening academic freedom.

The exact contrary is, in my judgment, the case as regards academic freedom in the popular sense, that is to say, of dictatorial interferences by moneyed benefactors with special individual utterances.

It does not follow, however, that there is no danger in the present situation. Academic freedom is not exhausted in the right to express opinion. More fundamental is the matter of freedom of work. Subtle and refined danger is always more to be apprehended than a public and obvious one. Encroachments that arise unconsciously out of the impersonal situation are more to be dreaded than those coming from the voluntary action of individuals. Influences that gradually sap and

undermine the conditions of free work are more ominous than those
which attack the individual in the open. Ability to talk freely is an important thing, but hardly comparable with ability to work freely. Now freedom of work is not a matter which lends itself to sensational newspaper
articles. It is an intangible, undefinable affair; something which is in the
atmosphere and operates as a continuous and unconscious stimulus. It
affects the spirit in which the university as a whole does its work, rather
than the overt expressions of any one individual. The influences which
help and hinder in this freedom are internal and organic, rather than
outward and personal.

Without being a pessimist, I think it behooves the community of
university men to be watchful on this side. Upon the whole, we are
pretty sure that actual freedom of expression is not going to be interrupted at the behest of any immediate outside influence, even if accom-
panied with the prospective gift of large sums of money. Things are too
far along for that. The man with money hardly dare directly interfere
with freedom of inquiry, even if he wished to; and no respectable university administration would have the courage, even if it were willing,
to defy the combined condemnation of other universities and of the
general public.

None the less the financial factor in the conduct of the modem university is continually growing in importance, and very serious problems
arise in adjusting this factor to strict educational ideals. Money is absolutely indispensable as a means. But it is only a means. The danger lies
in the difficulty of making money adequate as a means, and yet keeping
it in its place—not permitting it to usurp any of the functions of control
which belong only to educational purposes. To these, if the university is
to be a true university, money and all things connected therewith must
be subordinate. But the pressure to get the means is tending to make it
an end; and this is academic materialism—the worst foe of freedom of
work in its widest sense.

Garfield's conception of the college as a bench with a student at one
end and a great teacher at the other, is still a pious topic of after-dinner
reminiscence; but it is without bearing in the present situation. The
modem university is itself a great economic plant. It needs libraries,

museums, and laboratories, numerous, expensive to found and to maintain. It requires a large staff of teachers.

Now the need for money is not in itself external to genuine university concerns; much less antagonistic to them. The university must expand in order to be true to itself, and to expand it must have money. The danger is that means absorb attention and thus possess the value that attaches alone to the ultimate educational end. The public mind gives an importance to the money side of educational institutions which is insensibly modifying the standard of judgment both within and without the college walls. The great event in the history of an institution is now likely to be a big gift, rather than a new investigation or the development of a strong and vigorous teacher. Institutions are ranked by their obvious material prosperity, until the atmosphere of money-getting and money-spending hides from view the interests for the sake of which money alone has a place. The imagination is more or less taken by the thought of this force, vague but potent; the emotions are enkindled by grandiose conceptions of the possibilities latent in money. Unconsciously, without intention, the money argument comes to be an argument out of proportion, out of perspective. It is bound up in so many ways, seen and unseen, with the glory and dignity of the institution that it derives from association an importance to which it has in itself no claim.

This vague potentiality, invading imagination and seducing emotion, checks initiative and limits responsibility. Many an individual who would pursue his straight course of action unhindered by thought of personal harm to himself, is deflected because of fear of injury to the institution to which he belongs. The temptation is attractive just because it does not appeal to the lower and selfish motives of the individual, but comes clothed in the garb of the ideals of an institution. Loyalty to an institution, *esprit de corps*, is strong in the university, as in the army and navy. A vague apprehension of bringing harm upon the body with which one is connected is kept alive by the tendency of the general public to make no distinction between an individual in his personal and his professional capacity. Whatever he says and does is popularly regarded as an official expression of the institution with which he is connected. All this tends to paralyze independence and drive the individual back into a narrower comer of work.

Moreover, a new type of college administration has been called into being by the great expansion on the material side. A ponderous machinery has come into existence for carrying on the multiplicity of business and quasi-business matters without which the modem university would come to a standstill. This machinery tends to come between the individual and the region of moral aims in which he should assert himself. Personality counts for less than the apparatus thru which, it sometimes seems, the individual alone can accomplish anything. Moreover, the minutiae, the routine turning of the machinery, absorb time and energy. Many a modern college man is asking himself where he is to get the leisure and strength to devote himself to his ultimate ends, so much, willy-nilly, has to be spent on the intermediate means. The side-tracking of personal energy into the routine of academic machinery is a serious problem.

All this, while absorbing some of the energy which ought to find outlet in dealing with the larger issues of life, would not be so threatening were it not for its association with the contemporary tendency to specialization. Specialization, in its measure and degree, means withdrawal. It means preoccupation with a comparatively remote field in relatively minute detail. I have no doubt that in the long run the method of specialization will justify itself, not only scientifically, but practically. But value in terms of ultimate results is no reason for disguising the immediate danger to courage, and the freedom that can come only from courage. Teaching, in any case, is something of a protected industry; it is sheltered. The teacher is set somewhat one side from the incidence of the most violent stresses and strains of life. His problems are largely intellectual, not moral; his associates are largely immature. There is always the danger of a teacher's losing something of the virility that comes from having to face and wrestle with economic and political problems on equal terms with competitors. Specialization unfortunately increases these dangers. It leads the individual, if he follows it unreservedly, into bypaths still further off from the highway where men, struggling together, develop strength. The insidious conviction that certain matters of fundamental import to humanity are none of my concern because outside of my *Fach*, is likely to work more harm to genuine freedom of academic work than any fancied dread of interference from a moneyed benefactor.

The expansion of the material side of the modern university also carries with it strong tendencies towards centralization. The old-fashioned college faculty was pretty sure to be a thorough-going democracy in its way. Its teachers were selected more often because of their marked individual traits than because of pure scholarship. Each stood his own and for his own. The executive was but *primus inter pares*. It was a question not of organization or administration (or even of execution on any large scale), but rather of person making himself count in contact with person, whether teacher or student. All that is now changed—necessarily so. It requires ability of a very specialized and intensified order to wield the administrative resources of a modern university. The conditions make inevitably for centralization. It is difficult to draw the line between that administrative centralization which is necessary for the economical and efficient use of resources and that moral centralization which restricts initiative and responsibility. Individual participation in legislative authority and position is a guarantee of strong, free, and independent personalities. The old faculty, a genuine republic of letters, is likely to become an oligarchy-more efficient from the standpoint of material results achieved, but of less account in breeding men. This reacts in countless ways upon that freedom of work which is necessary to make the university man a force in the working life of the community. It deprives him of responsibility, and with weakening of responsibility comes loss of initiative.

This is one phase of the matter—fortunately not the whole of it. There has never been a time in the history of the world when the community so recognized its need of expert guidance as to-day. In spite of our intellectual chaos, in spite of the meaningless hullabaloo of opinion kept up so persistently about us by the daily press, there is a very genuine hunger and thirst after light. The man who has the word of wisdom to say is sure of his audience. If he gets his light out from under the bushel, it carries a long way. From this point of view there are strong influences working to free the university spirit, the spirit of inquiry and expression of truth, from its entanglements and concealments. The need being imperative, the stimulus is great. A due degree of courage, a due measure of the spirit of initiative and personal responsibility is the natural response. With the decay of external and merely governmental forms of authority, the demand grows for the authority of wisdom and intelligence. This force is bound to overcome those influences which tend to withdraw and pen the scholar within his own closet.

An immediate resource counteracting the dangers threatening academic freedom, is found also in the growth of intercollegiate sentiment and opinion. No fact is more significant than the growing inclination on the part of scientific associations to assume a right and duty to inquire into what affects the welfare of its own line of inquiry, however and wherever it takes place. This is the growth of the corporate scientific consciousness; the sense of the solidarity of truth. Whatever wounds the body of truth in one of its members attacks the whole organism. It is not chimerical to foresee a time when the consciousness of being a member of an organized society of truth-seekers will solidify and reenforce otherwise scattered and casual efforts.

Given that individual initiative whose permanent weakening we can scarcely imagine in an Anglo-Saxon community: and two forces, the need of the community for guidance and the sense of membership in the wider university to which every inquirer belongs, will assuredly amply triumph over all dangers attacking academic freedom.

What Is a University?

Robert M. Hutchins

A SPEECH DELIVERED BY THE PRESIDENT
OF THE UNIVERSITY OF CHICAGO

APRIL 18, 1935

Opening with a searing short paragraph combining terse, declarative refrain with a series of apophatic reproaches, Robert Hutchins comes out swinging in this public response to the Illinois state senate Paul Broyles's announcement of an investigation into the University. Like the first lyrics of an anthem, these lines are oft repeated within the University during times of challenge. In answer to the question posed by his title, Hutchins's distillation is pure, simple, and unforgettable: a community of scholars. This formulation emphasizes individual genius set within the synergistic context of academic community. Hanna Holborn Gray, who served as president from 1978 to 1993, wrote that Hutchins "set out deliberately to play the role of enfant terrible and revolutionary; indeed, he was to say that a president's function is precisely to be a troublemaker."[1] He certainly saw the stakes. "The American people must decide whether they will longer tolerate the search for truth. If they will, the universities will endure and give light and leading to the nation. If they will not . . . we can blow out the light and fight it out in the dark; for when the voice of reason is silenced, the rattle of machine gun begins."

A university is a community of scholars. It is not a kindergarten; it is not a club; it is not a reform school; it is not a political party; it is not an agency of propaganda. A university is a community of scholars.

The scholars who compose that community have been chosen by their predecessors because they are especially competent to study and to teach some branch of knowledge. The greatest university is that in which the largest proportion of these scholars are most competent in their chosen fields.

To a certain extent the ability of a university to attract the best scholars depends on the salaries it can pay. To a certain extent it depends on the facilities, the libraries and laboratories it can offer. But great scholars have been known to sacrifice both salaries and facilities for the sake of the one thing that is indispensable to their calling, and that is freedom.

Freedom of inquiry, freedom of discussion, and freedom of teaching—without these a university cannot exist. Without these a university becomes a political party or an agency of propaganda. It ceases to be a university. The university exists only to find and to communicate the truth. If it cannot do that it is no longer a university.

Socrates used to say that the one thing he knew positively was that we were under a duty to inquire. Inquiry involves still, as it did with Socrates, the discussion of all important problems and of all points of view. You will even find Socrates discussing communism in the *Republic* of Plato. The charge upon which Socrates was executed was the same that is now often hurled at our own educators: he was accused of corrupting the youth. The scholars of America are attempting in their humble way to follow the profession of Socrates. Some people talk as though they would like to visit upon them the fate which Socrates suffered. Such people should be reminded that the Athenians missed Socrates when he was gone.

There is nothing new about this issue in America. At the opening of the eighteenth century the foundation of Columbia University was delayed for fifty years because of arguments about what religious teaching should be permitted in the institution. Thereafter the fight was over the advance of experimental science and its repercussions on religious faiths. In the first ten years of the University of Chicago the quarrel turned on the religious teachings of the staff. The battle for freedom of inquiry and teaching in the natural sciences and religion has now been won. No sane citizen, however he may disagree with any professor, can wish that battle had been lost. The scientific advance of the past century and the release from bigotry which we now enjoy can be traced directly to the success of the universities in securing the right to study these fields without interference.

In the past forty years universities have taken up the study of economics, politics, sociology, and anthropology. They have been endeavoring to create social sciences, which if they can be created, may prove as beneficent to mankind as natural science and the technology which rests upon it. In inquiry into social problems professors have run into prejudices and fears, exactly as they did in studying natural science and theology.

These prejudices and fears are now especially intense, because we have been passing through a period of severe depression. In the twelve years I have been in higher education I have seen a marked change. In 1923 we often heard that the professor was a useless creature, remote from the real world and giving his students no knowledge of it. Now we hear that the professor should get back to the cloister and not let his students learn any more about the real world than he can help. I ascribe this change to the bad case of nerves induced in many people by the depression. The normal reaction to misfortune is to blame somebody else for it. Universities are easy marks. They are tax-exempt. They do not reply to abuse or misrepresentation. One who suffers from business cares, or domestic worries, or political disappointment, or general debility can relieve his feelings with impunity by talking about the Reds in the universities. I know that many honest and earnest people are seriously alarmed. I know, too, that they are misinformed.

As a matter of fact, I have never been able to find a Red professor. I have met many that were conservative, and some who would admit they were reactionary. I have met some who were not wholly satisfied with present conditions in this country. I have never met one who hoped to improve them through the overthrow of the government by force. The political and economic views of university faculties are those of a fair cross-section of the community. The views of those who are studying social problems are worth listening to, for these men are studying those problems in as unbiased and impartial a fashion as any human being can hope to study them.

When I was in college fifteen years ago students were the most conservative race of people in the country. Everybody lamented their indifference and apathy to the great questions of the day. I used to hear complaints that they read only the sporting pages of the newspapers and derived their other knowledge of current affairs from the movies. When I began to teach I taught a course called Introduction to Social Science. There were many aspects of the social sciences to which I could not introduce my class because they would not let me. The political and social dogmas then current these gentlemen had accepted whole. No suggestions of mine could sway or even arouse them.

At every age their elders have a way of overestimating the pliability of the young. As a result many people seem to have the notion that the student comes to college a sort of plastic mass, to be molded by the teacher in whatever likeness he will. But at 18, or 19, or graduation from high school, it is far too likely that the student has solidified, and too often in more ways than one. The most that a teacher can hope to do with such students is to galvanize or stimulate. If he wanted to, he could not hope to persuade.

It must be remembered that the purpose of education is not to fill the minds of students with facts; it is not to reform them, or amuse them, or make them expert technicians in any field. It is to teach them to think, if that is possible, and to think always for themselves. Democratic government rests on the notion that the citizens will think for themselves. It is of the highest importance that there should be some places where they can learn how to do it.

I have heard a great many times in recent years that more and more students were getting more and more Red. In universities that are intelligently conducted I do not believe it. In universities which permit students to study and talk as they please I see no evidence of increasing redness. The way to make students Red is to suppress them. This policy has never yet failed to have this effect. The vigorous and intelligent student resents the suggestion that he is not capable of considering anything more important than fraternities and football. Most of the college Reds I have heard about have been produced by the frightened and hysterical regulations of the colleges. They are not Reds at all; they are in revolt against being treated like children.

Mr. Thomas W. Lamont, partner in J.P. Morgan and Company, has advanced another reason for the interest of students in unconventional doctrines, a reason which is doubtless operating too. Mr. Lamont says, "I hear complaint that our college professors are teaching too much of socialistic theory. That would not be my observation. These are days," says Mr. Lamont, "when among the teaching forces. . . . The freest sort of academic freedom should prevail." He goes on: "But to me it is little wonder that many of our students today are radical, joining the Socialist Party, or are even looking with a kindly eye upon the allurements of Communism. The sort of world they have seen," says Mr. Lamont, "is one of chaos. . . ."

If Mr. Lamont is right, instead of attempting to suppress free discussion, we should set ourselves to remedy the cause of radicalism, the chaos of the modern world. I venture to suggest the value of encouraging intelligent, calm, and dispassionate inquiry into methods of bringing order out of chaos. That is the American way.

In the State of Illinois the Communist Party is on the ballot. Should students be allowed to graduate from Illinois colleges in ignorance of what Communism is? If they did they might vote that ticket by mistake. The greatest historian of the South has shown that the War between the States arose largely because the southern colleges and universities did not dare to say that there were any arguments against slavery and secession. Those who would suppress freedom of inquiry, discussion, and teaching are compelled to say that they know all the answers. Such a position is egregiously conceited. It is also a menace to our form of government. As Walter Lippmann has said, "The essence of the American system . . . is a way of life in which men proceed by unending inquiry and debate."

Anybody who has real familiarity with higher education will not hesitate to assert that professors are not engaged in subversive teaching. They will also remind the public that professors are citizens. They are not disfranchised when they take academic posts. They therefore enjoy all the rights of free speech, free thought, and free opinion that other citizens have. No university would permit them to indoctrinate their students with their own views. No university would permit them to turn the classroom into a center of propaganda. But off the campus, outside the classroom, they may hold or express any political or economic views that it is legal for an American to express or hold. Any university would be glad to have Mr. Einstein among its professors. Would anybody suggest that he should be discharged because he is a "radical"?

All parties, groups, and factions in this country should be interested in preserving the freedom of the universities. Some of our States now have radical administrations which have reached out to absorb the universities. The only hope in those States for the preservation of another point of view is in adhering to the doctrine that if a professor is a competent scholar he may hold his post, no matter how his political views differ from those of the majority. Not only so, the newspapers, the broadcasters, the churches, and every citizen should uphold the traditional rights of the scholar. Wherever freedom of inquiry, discussion, and teaching have been abolished freedom of the press, freedom of religion, and freedom of speech have been threatened or abolished, too.

Look at the universities of Russia and see how they have sunk to be mere mouthpieces of the ruling party. Look at the universities of Italy, where only those doctrines which the government approves may be expounded. Look at the universities of Germany, once among the greatest in the world, now a mere shadow, because their freedom is gone. These are the ways of communism and fascism.

In America we have had such confidence in democracy that we have been willing to support institutions of higher learning in which the truth might be pursued, and when found might be communicated to our people. We have not been afraid of the truth, or afraid to hope that it might emerge from the clash of opinion. The American people must decide whether they will longer tolerate the search for truth. If they will, the universities will endure and give light and leading to the nation. If they will not, then as a great political scientist has put it, we can blow out the light and fight it out in the dark; for when the voice of reason is silenced, the rattle of machine gun begins.

Broyles Commission Testimony

Robert M. Hutchins

APRIL 21, 1949

Rising to meet a second wave of Red Scare investigations in the post–World War II climate, Hutchins marshals his rhetorical skills to push back against forces of illiberalism in his testimony before the Illinois General Assembly's Broyles Commission. Chaired by State Senator Paul W. Broyles, the commission was active from 1947 to 1949 and introduced five bills into the state legislature. The so-called Broyles Bills (which Hutchins references) required loyalty oaths from public school teachers and many in civil service and mandated the firing of teachers deemed to be subversive of the state or federal government. Given the breadth of the commission's charge and the language in the statutes it passed, it is unsurprising that Hutchins addresses the dangers of guilt by association and presumption of subversive activity without any due process or actual evidence, as well as the futility of any attempt to suppress ideas. Hutchins also refers to the University's collaboration with the Manhattan Project and the team of physicists, led by Professor Enrico Fermi, who conducted the world's first controlled, self-sustaining nuclear chain reaction, under the stands of a football field. After the war, the University continued to operate the Metallurgical Laboratory, which Hutchins here refers to as the government's "principal laboratory of atomic research." Met Lab would become Argonne National Laboratory, a collaboration that continues between the Department of Energy and the University. Hutchins did not support the use of the atomic bomb, and appealed to President Truman to refrain from it.[1] While those attempts were kept from the public eye, his repudiation of McCarthyism was both open and vigorous: "The miasma of thought-control that is now spreading over the country is the greatest menace to the United States since Hitler."

My name is Robert M. Hutchins. I have been the chief executive officer of the University of Chicago for twenty years. The subpoena I have received summons me to testify concerning subversive activities at the University of Chicago. This is a leading question: The answer is assumed in the question. I cannot testify concerning subversive activities at the University of Chicago because there are none . . .

. . . The faculty of the University is, as everybody knows, one of the most distinguished in the world. The faculty numbers 1000. None of its members is engaged in subversive activities. The principal reason why the University has such a distinguished faculty is that the University guarantees its professors absolute and complete academic freedom. Nobody has ever ventured to say that any member of the faculty of the University of Chicago is a Communist. It has sometimes been said that some of the faculty belong to some so-called "communist front" organizations. The University of Chicago does not believe in the un-American doctrine of guilt by association. The fact that some Communists belong to, believe in, or even dominate some of the organizations to which some of our professors belong does not show that these professors are engaged in subversive activities. All that such facts would show would be that these professors believed in some of the objects of the organizations. It is entirely possible to belong to organizations combating fascism and racial discrimination, for example, without desiring to subvert the government of the United States.

The University has many thousands of students. None of them, so far as I know, is engaged in subversive activities. One of two students are alleged to have publicly said that they are communists. I am not aware that they have advocated the overthrow of the government by violence. If they have, they have broken the law of this State, and the proper officials should have proceeded against them.

As is well known, there is a Communist Club among the students of the University. Eleven students belong to it. The Club has not sought to subvert the government of this State. Its members claim that they are interested in studying Communism, and some of them, perhaps all of them, may be sympathetic towards Communism; but I do not see how the sympathetic feelings of eleven or a dozen students at the University of Chicago can be a danger to the State.

The policy of the University is to admit law-abiding students who have the qualifications to do the University work. It would not be in the public interest to exclude students of Communist leanings. If we did, how would they ever learn better? The policy of the University is to permit students to band together for any lawful purpose in terms of their common interests. This is conformable to the spirit of the Constitution of the United States, which guarantees free speech and the right of the people to peaceable assembly. There are 129 student clubs of one kind or another on the campus. Fourteen years ago a legislative committee attempted to find evidence of subversive activities at the University. You know that no evidence was found. There have been no changes since that would justify this investigation. Since the last investigation the University has been entrusted by the Government of the United States with the most momentous military secret in history. The first chain reaction took place on the campus of the University. The University today manages for the government its principal laboratory of atomic research. In addition the University is engaged in many other secret research projects on behalf of the defense establishment. The Government maintains a security officer on the campus. Because of the secret projects I have referred to, Federal agents constantly visit the campus. It is unlikely that if there were subversive activities there, they would not have reported them.

An investigator for this Commission spent days on the campus a year ago. Neither the Legislature nor the University has been informed that he discovered any subversive activities at the University. I can only conclude that he found none.

The resolution calling for this investigation originated in the House, of which the Chairman of this Commission is not a member. The reason given was that some hundreds of young people, about twenty percent of whom were students at the University of Chicago, demonstrated in an impolite manner against certain bills pending in the Legislature. The penalty does not seem to fit the crime. Rudeness and Redness are not the same. I recognize that it is provoking to the Legislature to be impolitely treated when it is conscientiously performing its duties. But even if I admitted that students of the University of Chicago were as impolite as they were alleged to have been, I could not admit that impoliteness was even presumptive evidence of subversive activities or that the fact that students were impolite showed that they had been taught to be impolite or subversive by the faculty of the University of Chicago.

The bills against which these students demonstrated were not so obviously perfect as to suggest that anybody who demonstrated against them was subversive or engaged in subversive acts. Three out of four newspapers in Chicago are opposed to these bills. These students exercised their right as American citizens to protest against pending legislation of which they disapproved. They were entirely right to disapprove of this pending legislation. The Broyles Bills are unnecessary since any dangers against which they are designed to protect us are already covered by laws now on the statute books. They are, in my opinion, as a former professor of law, unconstitutional. And, worst of all, they are un-American, since they aim at thought-control. They aim at the suppression of ideas. It is now fashionable to call anybody with whom we disagree a Communist or a fellow-traveler. So Branch Rickey darkly hinted the other day that the attempt to eliminate the reserve clause in baseball contracts was the work of Communists. One who criticizes the foreign policy of the United States, or the draft, or the Atlantic Pact, or who believes that our military establishment is too expensive, can be called a fellow-traveler, for the Russians are of the same opinion. One who thinks that there are too many slums and too much lynching in America can be called a fellow-traveler, for the Russians say the same. One who opposes racial discrimination or the Ku Klux Klan can be called a fellow-traveler, for the Russians claim that they ought to be opposed. Anybody who wants any change of any kind in this country can be called a fellow-traveler, because the Russians want change in this country, too.

The Constitution of the United States guarantees freedom of speech and right of the people peaceably to assemble. The American way has been to encourage thought and discussion. We have never been afraid of thought and discussion. The whole educational system, not merely the University of Chicago, is a reflection of the American faith in thought and discussion as the path to peaceful change and improvement. The danger to our institutions is not from the tiny minority who do not believe in them. It is from those who would mistakenly repress the free spirit upon which those institutions are built. The miasma of thought-control that is now spreading over the country is the greatest menace to the United States since Hitler. There are two ways of fighting subversive ideas. One is the policy of repression. This policy is contrary to the letter and spirit of the Constitution of this country. It cannot be justly enforced because it is impossible to tell precisely what people are thinking; they have to be judged by their acts. It has been generally thought that the widest possible latitude should be given to freedom of speech and publication, on the ground that the expression of differing points of view, some of which are bound to be unpopular, is the way to profess in the state. Hyde Park Corner in London, where anybody may say anything, has long been a symbol of the confidence of the Anglo-Saxon world in the ability of democratic institutions to withstand criticism, and even to nourish itself upon it. There are numerous laws already on the books which provide for the punishment of subversive acts.

The policy of repression of ideas cannot work and has never worked. The alternative to it is the long, difficult road of education. To this the American people have been committed. It requires patience and tolerance even in the face of intensive provocation. It requires faith that when the citizen understands all forms of government, he will prefer democracy and that he will be a better citizen if he is convinced than he would be if he were coerced. The Legislature and the University of Chicago are both opposed to Communism. The task of the Legislature is not merely to protect the people by passing laws that prevent the minority from overthrowing the state. It is to eliminate those social and economic evils and those political injustices which are the sources of discontent and disaffection. The members of the faculty of the University have many times assisted the Legislature in its efforts to discover and remedy these evils and injustices, and they are ready at all times to assist it.

The task of the University is to enlighten the community, to provide citizens who know the reasons for their faith and who will be a bulwark to our democracy because they have achieved conviction through study and thought. The University does not claim that it is perfect or that it always succeeds. It asserts, however, that the policy of education is better than the policy of repression and that it is earnestly dedicated to making the policy of education produce the results that the American people have believed it can produce. All the University asks of the Legislature, and all it has ever asked of it, is a sympathetic understanding of this task.

In the cross examination immediately following this statement, it was established that the Communist Club has a membership of eleven and that all members are listed in the Dean's office.

Are We Afraid of Freedom?

Laird Bell

A STATEMENT FROM THE CHAIRMAN OF THE
UNIVERSITY OF CHICAGO BOARD OF TRUSTEES

APRIL 11, 1949

This statement is unique in this collection, as it was penned by a chair of the University of Chicago Board of Trustees, rather than by a scholar or administrator. Laird Bell was a prominent lawyer and civic leader in Chicago, who worked closely with Robert Hutchins during his tenure. As the McCarthy era was cresting, the Illinois legislature instigated investigations of "subversive activities," led by State Senator Paul Broyles. This piece, along with the ensuing faculty statement "On Academic Freedom," are the University's response to what came to be known as the Broyles affair. The two statements are best read together and notable in their distinct points of emphasis. "Are We Afraid of Freedom?" asserts that the trustees and administration of the University oppose communism as a force seeking to suppress the free exchange of ideas. It offers supporting arguments for that assertion, along with a historical walk-through of major touchstones of free speech, from John Milton to Dwight D. Eisenhower. Furthermore, Bell asserts that "there is no communist professor at the University of Chicago," and "no Communist indoctrination . . . in any course or program in its curriculum." Besides the factual absence among the faculty and curricula, Bell's case is that communism is simply antithetical to the university's atmosphere of free and open inquiry, and thus has no potential of taking root. In other words, there is nothing to fear from freedom.

It has been well said . . . that "Chicago is proud of its University, one of
the greatest in the world." . . . We have become thoroughly convinced by
this investigation that one of the greatest safeguards for the perpetuation of American idealism and American institutions lies in the absolute
scholastic freedom of our universities and that the University of Chicago
is an admirable example of how that freedom should be exercised. . . .
Any action on our part which would even indirectly hamper that scholastic freedom which our schools enjoy would indeed be subversive of the
very principles underlying our form of government.

—MAJORITY REPORT
Illinois State Legislative Committee authorized to investigate the
University of Chicago, June 26, 1935

In 1935 the Legislature of the State of Illinois empowered a committee
to investigate alleged seditious activities at the University of Chicago.
Charges were made. Damaging surmises were printed in the public
press. The work of the University was interrupted. At the conclusion of
the investigation the committee wrote in its report:

Has the University of Chicago or any of its professors violated either the
letter or the spirit of our laws? The answer to this question must be in the
negative. . . . *Nothing in the teachings or schedule of the school can be held to be subversive of our institutions or the advocation of the communist form of government
as a substitution for the present form of government of the United States.*

The committee cleared the University. But a university is dependent on the public's appraisal of its contribution, and harm had already
been done. Even the generosity of Mr. Walgreen, who contributed five
hundred and fifty thousand dollars to the University after the investigation was closed, did not remove the impression created by the headline
charges.

A serious question is again raised by an investigating committee of
the Illinois Legislature. The question is fundamental to democracy. It
underlies all scholarship and all thoughtful inquiry. Therefore, it underlies the very purpose of a great university. The question is this: In these
troubled times are we afraid of freedom?

This year on March 1, 1949, a group of students from Illinois universities, including a number of students from the University of Chicago, traveled to Springfield to protest the five bills introduced into the state legislature by Senator Paul Broyles. This they had the right to do. If they were disorderly, we disapprove of their conduct. Immediately following this student protest, House Joint Resolution No. 21 was passed calling for an investigation of the University and stating: "It appears that these students are being indoctrinated with Communistic and other subversive theories contrary to our free systems of representative government. . . ." This resolution was passed within a few minutes, without customary hearings or referral to committee.

So, once again apparently the University is to be "investigated." Once again statements harmful to the University's reputation have been made. We think that the people who have made these statements do not know the facts. Most of the statements are untrue. But the newspaper reader is likely to assume that "where there's smoke, there's fire." Therefore, this statement is being made. The truth does not lie somewhere between the allegations of irresponsible individuals and our statement of it. The facts spell the truth, and the truth is the opposite of the charges.

There is no Communist professor at the University of Chicago. There is no Communist indoctrination at the University of Chicago in any course or program in its curriculum.

We know that there is a Communist Club at the University—one of some two hundred student organizations. We know also that its membership comprises one-tenth of 1 percent of the total student body, about one out of every thousand. The Board, which controls and directs the affairs of this University, could refuse to recognize that organization. But we believe with Mr. Justice Oliver Wendell Holmes that "with effervescent opinions . . . the quickest way to let them get flat is to let them get exposed to the air."

Communism is a term which is used loosely by different people to mean different things. Not everyone who advocates change is a Communist. In times when there is fear of Communist infiltration many persons are afraid of any criticism of things as they are. There is a tendency at such times to put a "red" label on anyone with whose opinions one may not agree. Universities have as much duty to defend the free expression of opinion within the bounds of legality as they have to prevent what is illegal. If such defense subjects the University to the harassment of a legislative investigation and to the possibility of inadequate or distorted reports of it, we shall nevertheless defend the University's principles with all the vigor we can command.

The Tradition of Individual Freedom

The Trustees and Administration of this University are against communism. They are against it because, among other reasons, it is contrary to our free tradition. Communism suppresses ideas. We oppose communism as we oppose all efforts to undermine our constitutionally guaranteed free speech, free press, and free assembly. We oppose communism because we believe in the tradition of individual freedom which men throughout the centuries have fought to preserve. This tradition has been stated by many men in many ways. A few of these statements follow:

JOHN MILTON
   Areopagitica, 1644

Give me the liberty to know, to utter, and to argue freely according to conscience, above all liberties. . . . And though all the winds of doctrine were let loose to play upon the earth, so Truth be in the field, we do injuriously by licensing and prohibiting to misdoubt her strength. Let her and Falsehood grapple; who ever knew Truth put to the worse, in a free and open encounter?

THOMAS JEFFERSON
   "First Inaugural Address," 1801

If there be any among us who wish to dissolve this union, or change its republican form, let them stand undisturbed, as monuments of the safety with which error of opinion may be tolerated where reason is left free to combat it.

JOHN STUART MILL
   On Liberty, 1859

This, then, is the appropriate region of human liberty. It comprises, first, the inward domain of consciousness; demanding liberty of conscience, in the most comprehensive sense; liberty of thought and feeling; absolute freedom of opinion and sentiment on all subjects, practical or speculative, scientific, moral, or theological.

WOODROW WILSON
   "Message to Congress," 1919

The only way to keep men from agitating against grievances is to remove the grievances. An unwillingness even to discuss these matters produces only dissatisfactions and gives comfort to the extreme elements in our country which endeavor to stir up disturbances in order to provoke Governments to embark upon a course of retaliation and repression. The seed of revolution is repression.

OLIVER WENDELL HOLMES
   Abrams v. United States, 1919

But when men have realized that time has upset many fighting faiths, they may come to believe even more than they believe the very foundations of their own conduct that the ultimate good desired is better reached by free trade in ideas—that the best test of truth is the power of the thought to get itself accepted in the competition of the market. . . .

LOUIS D. BRANDEIS
   Gilbert v. Minnesota, 1920

The right of a citizen of the United States to take part, for his own or the country's benefit, in the making of federal laws and in the conduct of the government, necessarily includes the right to speak or write about them; to endeavor to make his own opinion concerning laws existing or contemplated prevail; and to this end, to teach the truth as he sees it. . . . Like the course of the heavenly bodies, harmony in national life is a resultant of the struggle between contending forces. In frank expression of conflicting opinion lies the greatest promise of wisdom in governmental action; and in suppression lies ordinarily the greatest peril.

CHARLES EVANS HUGHES
Letter to Speaker Sweet of the New York State Legislature, reported in the *New York Times*, January 10, 1920

If public officers or private citizens have any evidence that any individual or group of individuals are plotting revolution and seeking by violent measures to change our Government, let the evidence be laid before the proper authorities and swift action be taken for the protection of the community. Let every resource of inquiry, of pursuit, of prosecution be employed to ferret out and punish the guilty according to our laws. But I count it a most serious mistake to proceed, not against individuals charged with violation of law, but against masses of our citizens combined for political action, by denying them the only resource of peaceful government: that is, action by the ballot box and through duly elected representatives in legislative bodies.

ALFRED E. SMITH
In his message vetoing the Lusk Laws, which sought to license schools and to require teachers' oaths, 1919

Its avowed purpose is to safeguard the institutions and traditions of the country. In effect, it strikes at the very foundation of one of the most cardinal institutions of our nation—the fundamental right of the people to enjoy full liberty in the domain of idea and speech. To this fundamental right there is and can be under our system of government but one limitation, namely, that the law of the land shall not be transgressed, and there is abundant statute law prohibiting the abuse of free speech. . . . The profound sanity of the American people has been demonstrated in many a crisis, and I, for one, do not believe that governmental dictation of what may and may not be taught is necessary to achieve a continuance of the patriotism of our citizenship and its loyal support of the government and its institutions.

The Tradition Continues

Opinions such as these are often unpopular, especially when they are spoken in times of stress. But they have been stated again and again by men who were not isolated thinkers but men of action. It is fortunate that in the midst of our present apprehensions and alarms America does not lack men of the courage to continue the democratic tradition.

ROBERT A. TAFT
"The Battle Against Communism," address to the Executives Club of Milwaukee, May 8, 1948

There has been a good deal of talk of outlawing the Communist Party. Of course, under our Constitution, we cannot and should not make it illegal for an American citizen to think communism or express his opinions as long as he does not advocate a violent overthrow of the government. We cannot afford, if we are going to maintain freedom in this country, to violate the Constitution. We would be killing the very liberty which it is the purpose of our whole policy to preserve against totalitarian attack.

DWIGHT D. EISENHOWER
Installation Address as President of Columbia University, the expression of his administrative policy, October 12, 1948

There will be no administrative suppression or distortion of any subject that merits a place in this University's curricula. The facts of communism, for instance, shall be taught here—its ideological development, its political methods, its economic effects, its probable course in the future. The truth about communism is, today, an indispensable requirement if the true values of our democratic system are to be properly assessed. Ignorance of communism, fascism, or any other police-state philosophy is far more dangerous than ignorance of the most virulent disease.

Who among us can doubt the choice of future Americans, as between statism and freedom, if the truth concerning each be constantly held before their eyes? But if we, as adults, attempt to hide from the young the facts in this world struggle, not only will we be making a futile attempt to establish an intellectual "iron curtain," but we will arouse the lively suspicion that statism possesses virtues whose persuasive effect we fear.

WILBUR J. BENDER
   Dean of Harvard College, in the March, 1949, issue of the *Harvard Alumni Bulletin* answered those who criticized Harvard for permitting Gerhart Eisler to speak before the John Reed Society

I know of no faster way of producing communists than by making martyrs out of the handful of communists we now have. Forbidding them to speak would be not only treason to the ancient traditions of Harvard and America: It would be proof that we have something to hide, that we have lost faith in our principles and in our way of life. It would be accepting communist practices in the name of Americanism . . . I devoutly hope that the time will never come when we are faced with the sorry spectacle of a great University and a great country trembling timorously in fear of the words of a communist or of a demagogic commentator.

What About Spies?

Today, some men devoted to freedom are worried about spies. They would "get rid of all the reds" to eliminate the possibility of espionage. We, too, are against spies. But not everyone who is called "red" is a spy. And, more important, not all spies announce themselves as "reds." The danger, if any, does not exist with the noisy agitators. The University of Chicago is engaged in secret projects of vital importance to national defense. The University is under surveillance of professional investigators, agents of the F.B.I. and of the military intelligence units. This, we think, is the way to look for spies. The general suppression of "reds" is too simple, too amateurish to be effective. J. Edgar Hoover, head of the F.B.I., is against it.

The Atomic Bomb

"The Italian navigator has landed in the New World, and the natives are friendly."

In this cryptic message, so legend has it, the news of Enrico Fermi's successful operation of the atomic "pile" under the grandstand of Stagg Field at the University of Chicago was flashed to Washington on December 2, 1942. It meant that the chain reaction worked, and the first unleashing of atomic energy was under control.

The chain reaction made possible the most terrible weapon in history. It created the greatest economic fact of our time. It opened up endless new vistas for scientific accomplishment.

The work on the atomic bomb took great scientists. It also took great courage. Had it failed, the University might have been charged with the most spectacular boondoggle of all time. Or without the adequate calculations and protections which its scientists provided, the University might have been responsible for blowing up the northern end of Illinois.

The chain reaction is in a sense only a symbol of the working of freedom in ideas. It is no accident that the world's leading scientists wish to work in the free atmosphere provided by a great university. Freedom is the necessary condition of learning and progress.

Its contribution to the successful production of the atomic bomb was but one facet of the University's wartime activity. Its alumni and its staff served valiantly. It provided numerous trained individuals for positions of grave responsibility. Its facilities were mobilized and its activities ranged from interpretation and training in Chinese dialects and the prediction of weather in the Arctic region to the development of numerous protective measures for armed forces personnel. The University of Chicago has been honored by the Secretary of War for "contributing materially to the successful conclusion of World War II."

The Market Place of Free Ideas

> This University was founded and rose to international prominence under circumstances which are possible only in a free and democratic state. Free interchange of ideas, free research, and the right of its faculty members to engage without restraint in the activities dictated by their judgment and their conscience have been protected and encouraged. Out of this freedom have come the renowned contributions of this University to the humanities and to the physical sciences, the social sciences, and the biological sciences. The galaxy of Midwest state universities—Illinois, Michigan, Minnesota, Iowa—could scarcely have come to their current high standards without the compelling influence of the University of Chicago.
>
> —Edwin R. Embree, *Harper's Magazine*, March, 1949

It was in an atmosphere of freedom that A. A. Michelson, earliest American physicist to win the Nobel Prize, measured the diameter of a star for the first time; James H. Breasted, America's first professor of Egyptology, furthered the understanding and reconstruction of ancient society; Robert A. Millikan won the Nobel Prize for measuring the charge of the electron; Edgar J. Goodspeed achieved the status of the nation's foremost New Testament scholar; Arno Luckhardt discovered ethylene gas, used as an anesthetic in millions of operations; Frank Billings demonstrated that teeth and tonsils can be focal centers for the spread of infection; Arthur H. Compton won the Nobel Prize for his pioneer work on X-rays; Charles Merriam rose to eminence as a scholar and teacher of American political thought; Arthur J. Dempster isolated uranium 235, the atomic explosive—these men and the host of their distinguished colleagues produced the achievements which have placed this University among the foremost in the world.

Some day I would like to take a year off, return to Chicago, and write a book about the University of Chicago, which by any reckoning is one of the three or four most outstanding in the world.

—John Gunther, *Inside USA*

It is in that freedom that the men of the University work today to find a cure for cancer, to harness atomic energy for peaceful productive use, to widen our knowledge of the social, political, and cultural forces in all human experience, and to train the teachers, the scientists, the scholars, and the enlightened citizens of tomorrow. It is upon that freedom that the future promise of the University is dependent. As Norman Cousins, editor of the *Saturday Review of Literature*, wrote in an editorial:

> For it is that environment rather than any dogma that represents the real Chicago Story. It is impossible to spend any time on the campus without sensing the vitality of true academic freedom—not the academic freedom which limits itself (instead of being limited from without) to stump speeches or political activity, but the academic freedom which Holmes used to call the open marketplace of ideas. The spirit of independence, particularly as it applies to research . . . gives Chicago both its dominant characteristics and its chief claim on the future.

To be great, a university must adhere to principle. It cannot shift with the winds of passing public opinion. Its work is frequently mystifying and frequently misunderstood. It must rely for its support upon a relatively small number of people who understand the important contributions it makes to the welfare of the community and the improvement of mankind; upon those who understand that academic freedom is important not because of its benefits to professors but because of its benefits to all of us.

Today our tradition of freedom is under attack. There are those who are afraid of freedom. We do not share these fears. The University of Chicago needs the support of those who believe as we do.

On Academic Freedom

A STATEMENT ADOPTED BY THE COMMITTEE OF THE
COUNCIL UPON SUBMISSION BY EDWARD H. LEVI

JULY 12, 1949

One easily imagines that while Laird Bell was preparing his statement on behalf of
the Board of Trustees, a young law professor who would come to make indelible
contributions to the Chicago tradition was penning his own statement, on behalf
of the faculty. Edward H. Levi was monumentally influential on the University
and the country. Much of the writing and editing of this canon has taken place in
the building named in his honor. Shortly after writing this statement, Levi would
become dean of the Law School; twenty years later he would ascend to the office of University president before being tapped to serve as attorney general of
the United States by President Gerald R. Ford. The distinctiveness of the faculty
voice here—especially contrasted with that of the trustees through Bell's "Are We
Afraid of Freedom?"—is unmistakable. Whereas Bell's position rests on the factual
absence of any communist professors and the impossibility of communism taking root at the University, the faculty here declare that were any faculty members
communists, it would be fully protected by the academic freedom they enjoy, and
wholly immaterial to their competence and worthiness as scholars. But then they
go further. Were any competent and otherwise desirable faculty members who
happen to be communist at any other university deprived of appointment, promotion, or terminated because of their political beliefs, they would be welcome at
the University of Chicago. The faculty openly urge the administration to approve
appointments of such candidates. Give us your tired, your poor, your meritorious

scholars simply yearning to be free. Our welcome mat is out for you, and our only criterion for admission is academic excellence.

Various attempts are now being made throughout the United States to bar all communists from university faculties, and to impose on teachers special loyalty oaths or loyalty investigations. The Council believes that such proposals are misguided and constitute a serious threat to academic freedom.

These proposals go beyond a proper insistence that teachers and research workers should obey the law. They make activities or associations otherwise legal the basis for disqualification and deny to teachers the political rights possessed by other citizens. This loss of rights is not made necessary by security requirements for military secrets. These have been effectively enforced in the past without restricting academic freedom generally.

A widely accepted argument in favor of the exclusion of communists is that all communists adhere to a dogma and are required to accept political direction of their activities. Therefore it is said that since communists do not possess intellectual freedom, their exclusion cannot impair academic freedom. To this argument we answer that any such conclusive presumption about a group when applied to individuals does work a serious impairment of academic freedom. This impairment is both unnecessary and unwise.

It is unnecessary because the proper test for membership in the academic community is intellectual competence and integrity. This requires a willingness to engage in rational discussion, to question principles, and to subject conclusions reached in the field of scholarly endeavor to the searching test of scientific inquiry. This test places the emphasis where it belongs; namely, on the competence and intellectual freedom of the particular scholar. It eschews any conclusive presumptions which may operate to bar an individual because he is a member of a particular group. At the same time it recognizes that a man who adheres to a rigid set of tenets in political, historical, and economic theory may have a perfectly open and competent mind in some other field; for instance, physics, chemistry, or biology, which may be his field of academic activity. If it is true that all communists lack intellectual freedom, this test will operate to bar all communists from the academic community. On the other hand, it is contrary to the traditions of American education and democracy to exclude qualified scholars because of the application of a general proposition which in the individual case can be shown to be wrong.

We believe it is an unwise precedent for universities to bow to a popular demand that a particular minority group be excluded from the academic community. The road suggested by such proposals is the road which in the past has led to the exclusion of Catholics, Jews, scientists, and indeed all groups which may, at the time and place, be unpopular with the majority. Many pressures may make it expedient for a university to accede to such demands. University administrators may find it convenient to have a rule of thumb excluding all known communists without the necessity for any inquiry into individual competence and integrity. But academic freedom is too important to be subordinated to expediency and convenience.

Proposals which would automatically bar all communists from universities or require special loyalty oaths have the further defect that they will not accomplish the purposes for which they are sought. Communists seeking university employment, once such proposals have been adopted, will avoid formal party affiliations, and will engage in further concealment of their activities. Loyalty oaths then provide no deterrence. Automatic disqualifications provide no security. Rules of thumb must give way to investigation and loyalty proceedings. The evidence presented ceases to be proof of formal membership in the Communist Party. It becomes evidence of associations and the espousal of ideas which a reviewing committee might take as sympathy for communist views. An atmosphere of intellectual freedom cannot be preserved if men of integrity and competence are to be subjected to punishment or loyalty proceedings because of the ideas they hold.

The present attack on the universities is the more tragic because the instruments with which to combat communism and all other doctrines denying the integrity of the individual are to be found precisely in that freedom of inquiry and scientific spirit which have made American universities great. The answer to wrong ideas is not suppression but is to be found in their examination by free minds guided by competence and integrity. This undoubtedly is the reason why the number of communists in American universities today is small indeed.

It is to be feared that a number of our universities will be unable to resist the increasing pressure, and that men, who have violated no law, will be forced to resign or will be dismissed or refused appointment solely because in the public mind they have become identified with communist activities. If there should be among these men any who, by virtue of their scholarly competence and intellectual freedom and integrity, would appear to make desirable members of the faculty of the University of Chicago, and if their appointment is recommended by the appropriate departments, the Council will urge the Administration to approve such appointments.

It is of the utmost importance that political dictation of American universities be resisted. Each concession for reasons of expediency encourages new encroachments and makes further resistance more difficult. A great deal of collaboration between the government and the universities has been accomplished both in order to further military defense and to provide the fruits of education to the widest possible number of citizens. The basis for such collaboration, however, must be the understanding that political requirements, outside of the area of military secrets, may not be attached to membership in the university community and may not control the administration of the affairs of the university.

Inaugural Convocation Address

Edward H. Levi, President of the University of Chicago

NOVEMBER 14, 1968

As he took to the podium at Rockefeller Chapel to deliver his first formal address as president, Edward Levi openly disclosed his anxiety, which reflected the moment on campus and more broadly in the country. Student protesters were present as he gave his address and interrupted several speakers at his inaugural dinner. In this atmosphere of impending crisis, Levi, perhaps more than any of his predecessors, is explicit in describing the awesome tradition and values of the University and the virtues it seeks to practice. Three-quarters of a century into the University's founding, Levi's language articulates and exemplifies the crystallization of the Chicago tradition—he evinces reflexivity in recognizing that there is in fact a tradition, and that it has its own values and virtues. It is at this moment that he can more fully speak of a tradition that "is our inheritance." Beyond the responsibility that comes with the gift of this inheritance, Levi acknowledges the civil strife and tensions of the period. At times presaging dynamics that would greatly accelerate in the decades to follow, he notes the correlation of mass communication and the potential for distortion of public understanding. He laments the concomitant growth in the complexity of social problems, while the limits of knowledge are "agonizingly apparent in matters of public policy." Levi forcefully asserts moral aspects to the "corporate neutrality of the University on public policy issues," echoing the Kalven report, issued just one year earlier. However, his rhetoric anchors in the depth of the tradition, quoting William Rainey Harper's address of 1900 and the non-"disputant" principle of corporate neutrality. And yet, Levi clearly differentiates between that explicitly moral, principled position governing the University qua university, and his own denunciation; dropped into the address is a singular sentence, punctuated as its own paragraph: "The outrage of this war continues."

I trust I will be forgiven a personal word. I approach this unlikely moment with many memories. I come to it also with understandable concern. I do not misconceive the importance of this office, which has changed through the years. Rather, the goals, achievement and tradition of this University are disturbingly impressive. Our University has had a standard of extraordinary leadership, difficult to maintain. I am grateful to Chancellor Hutchins, Chancellor Kimpton and President Beadle for their presence today. They will understand my anxiety. It is not that we fear mistakes. Perhaps we should fear not to make them. President Hutchins in his address—given forty years ago—spoke of the University's experimental attitude, its willingness to try out ideas, to undertake new ventures, to pioneer. In some cases, he said, the contribution was to show other universities what not to do. Let me say, with rueful pride, since that time we have made many similar contributions. I hope we always will.

It is natural for this University to believe it believes in pioneering. After all, this University came into being as a pioneering first modern University, borrowing ideas from Germany and England, building upon the New England college, joining undergraduate instruction and a panoply of graduate research in what, some said, surely would be a monstrosity—all this done with Middle Western enthusiasm and a confidence the best could be obtained here if only it could be paid for. Much has been written of the financial arrangements of those days, the creative use of material resources generously given. But the basic faith was not in material resources. The faith was in the intellectual powers of the mind. It was considered important, more important than anything else in the world, to uncover and understand the cultures of the past, to appreciate the works of the mind, to penetrate the mysteries of the universe, to know more about the environment, the societies and the nature of man. The University's seriousness of purpose was proven from the first by its insistence upon freedom of inquiry and discussion. Intellectual tests for truth made other standards irrelevant. Schools for the propagation of special points of view might exist, Harper wrote, but they could not be called universities. The emphasis on the need to question and reexamine, both as part of the inquiry of research and the inquiry of teaching, established a basic unity for all of the University. The basis of that unity underscored the relationship between teaching and research. That unity encouraged discussion among disciplines. It supported the individual scholar as he crossed accepted boundaries of knowledge. It made possible—even compelled—continuing debate concerning the place of professional, specialized, general and liberal education within the University. It made the University self-critical.

"On an occasion such as this," as Mr. Kimpton stated on a similar occasion, "the important roles are not played by those who are present. . . . Our efforts are given importance by the opportunities and responsibilities . . . we inherit." So I have stressed those virtues which from the beginning and until now have characterized our institution: a willingness to experiment, a commitment for the intellectual search for truth, freedom of inquiry, and a concern for the educational process as though the freedom of man depended upon it. This is our inheritance. It is an inheritance preserved and strengthened, indeed made possible, by the action and faith of many who are present today.

We meet in a time of great difficulty. The society is divided. The conditions of public discussion have changed. More people can take part and react because they can be reached. Both the numbers involved and the means of communication increase the likelihood—and certainly the powers—of distortion. The problems are complex; the limits of knowledge are agonizingly apparent in matters of public policy. Meanwhile the investigations of the social sciences have made clearer the non-rational components of human behavior. The relevance and integrity of reason are questioned at the same time as impatience emphasizes the manipulative aspects of concepts and institutions.

The outrage of this war continues.

The view of the world as it is or could be is conditioned for many by the protective walls or barriers of higher education. Formal education at both the college and graduate level is highly regarded as the gateway to success. More than 45 percent of our young people in the applicable age group are in college—an extraordinary change and, with some qualifications, an extraordinary achievement. But the joyous news that the bank of knowledge is overstuffed, and can be drawn upon only with the assistance of the latest generation of computers, adds to the impression of a technical industrialized society in which individual thought and concern are powerless—in which basic decisions appear to have been made in other times or by other people in other places. The very idea that centers of education are for thoughtful, and therefore personal, consideration of values, and for increased understanding, is lost by those who insist that universities are mechanisms of service to be used in a variety of ways for the interests of the larger community.

There are many institutions for service in our society. Centers of learning and instruction have considerable difficulty in performing their central tasks; one may question the wisdom of assigning to them additional duties. In any event, among colleges, schools and universities there are important differences. Our history, capacity and objectives are not all the same. Each institution must find its own mission.

The mission of the University of Chicago is primarily the intellectual search for truth and the transmission of intellectual values. The emphasis must be on the achievement of that understanding which can be called discovery. President Beadle has spoken, as is his special right to do, of "the incomparable thrill of original discovery." He has referred to the importance of having students participate in the process through which knowledge is reaffirmed and additions to knowledge are made. This, of course, is the process of education—whatever the means used, and it applies to the dialogue as well as to the experiment. We should reaffirm the close connection between the creativity of teaching and the creativity of research. And we should reaffirm also our commitment to the way of reason, without which a University becomes a menace and a caricature.

It is of course easy to be in favor of reason. But the commitment is somewhat more demanding and difficult. President Harper in his decennial report took occasion to emphasize "that the principle of complete freedom of speech on all subjects has from the beginning been regarded as fundamental to The University of Chicago." At the same time he repeated the policy that "The University, as such, does not appear as a disputant on either side upon any public question and . . . utterances which any professor may make in public are to be regarded as representing his opinion only." Academic freedom is stronger now than it was then. But the propriety of the corporate neutrality of the University on public policy issues having moral aspects has been seriously challenged. The position questions the power or persuasiveness of ideas in themselves, recognizes the superior authority of official certification, or places reliance on other forms of power. Perhaps the position reflects the kind of frustration described by Louis Wirth in 1936. Professor Wirth wrote:

> At a time in human history like our own, when all over the world people are not merely ill at ease but are questioning the bases of social existence, the validity of their truths, and the tenability of their norms, it should become clear that there is no value apart from interest and no objectivity apart from agreement. Under such circumstances it is difficult to hold tenaciously to what one believes to be the truth in the face of dissent, and one is inclined to question the very possibility of an intellectual life. Despite the fact that the Western world has been nourished by a tradition of hard-won intellectual freedom and integrity for over two thousand years, men are beginning to ask whether the struggle to achieve these was worth the cost if so many today accept complacently the threat to exterminate what rationality and objectivity have been won in human affairs. The widespread depreciation of the value of thought, on the one hand, and its regression, on the other, are ominous signs of the deepening twilight of modern culture.

The issue raised is central to what a university should be and what it should stand for. It is of course quite true that the ideas of individual scholars in universities are not likely to immediately sway the world, although some have had considerable effect. The tasks which university faculty have undertaken, sometimes within, sometimes without the universities should not obscure the fact that universities exist for the long run. They are the custodians not only of the many cultures of man, but of the rational process itself. Universities are not neutral. They do exist for the propagation of a special point of view; namely, the worthwhileness of the intellectual pursuit of truth—using man's highest powers, struggling against the irrelevancies which corrupt thought, and now standing against the impatience of those who have lost faith in reason. This view does not remove universities from the problems of society. It does not diminish, indeed it increases, the pressure for the creation and exchange of ideas, popular or unpopular, which remake the world. It does suggest that the greatest contribution of universities will be in that liberation of the mind which makes possible what Kenneth Clark has called, the strategy of truth. "For," as he says, "the search for truth, while impotent without implementation in action, undergirds every other strategy in behalf of constructive social change." One would hope that this liberation of the mind would result from a liberal education at Chicago at both the undergraduate and graduate level.

One can well understand the impatience of those who prefer a different relevance of practical action. In some areas, implementation, leading to a more basic examination of consequences and meaning, has been made an appropriate part of training and research. But this may be insufficient to satisfy those who for the time being at least, and for laudable and understandable reasons, would prefer a different way of life. Nevertheless they stay within the educational system caught by its pretense and rigidity. They feel they must stay a long time. Not only has the number of years required for formal education steadily increased as college and graduate work are treated as necessities, but the model presses for the total absorption of the student's interest either in the curriculum or in ancillary activities. We are set on a course which suggests that every young person up to the age of twenty-five, every young family really, should have an educational institution as a surrogate for the world. Quite apart from the fact that institutions of higher learning should not be surrogates for the world, the satisfaction with which this development is greeted should be tempered. This development in part is a response to distortions caused by the Selective Service System. Much of the education at the graduate level—in some areas, not all—is unnecessary, or even worse is disqualifying for professional work, as for example the undergraduate teaching for which it is required. I do not expect agreement on that and I am probably wrong. For some areas I doubt whether the extended time can be justified as a reflection of the increase in knowledge. Rather, it appears as an unimaginative response on the part of the educational system to the existence of increased leisure time within the economy. And if the goal of a college education for everyone is to be met in a way to do the most good, the purposes and ways of that education, even the period of time involved, should be reexamined. I realize this has been done before, but perhaps it will not hurt too much to take another look. What I am trying to suggest is that for those who are interested in pioneering, there is much to think about. The University is a member of many communities. We cherish the relationship with other universities. We are a member of their world community. We are also an urban university on the South Side of Chicago. In many ways through many activities various members of the University faculties and students are working within the community. We seek to be a good neighbor. Most of us are in fact neighbors. The community has much to offer us. The fact that most of our faculty live here has helped to maintain the oneness and interdisciplinary character of this institution. It has made it possible to measure the effect of new enterprises and responsibilities upon the institution as a whole. This guideline enforces self restraint. It is, I think, of benefit both to the community and to the University. New models for pediatric care, for counselling and psychiatric assistance, and new approaches to the major problems of urban education should emerge from the endeavors which have been planned and developed with representatives of the community. These are not the only scholarly-service-training activities in which members of the faculty are engaged within the community which have significance far beyond the problems of one neighborhood and which over time may well determine the quality of life in world urban centers. The work in the complex problems of communities within the city is an encouraging continuation of historic research begun fifty years ago by the Chicago school of sociology.

In 1902 President Harper referred to the firmly established policy of the trustees "that to the faculties belong to the fullest extent the care of educational administration." "The responsibility," he said, "for the settlement of educational questions rests with the faculty." On this policy the initial greatness of the University was built. The trustees, whether they agreed or not with particular decisions, have been the strongest advocates of this policy. And the faculty have fulfilled this responsibility, protecting on the one hand the freedom of the individual scholar, and shepherding at the same time, although not without some pain, some of the most interesting programs for both undergraduate and graduate instruction attempted in this country. I stress the position of the faculty because obviously the quality of this University rests upon them and is created by them. And the burdens upon them have increased because the conditions of education have changed. Sir Eric Ashby in a notable address at the University of Witwatersrand quoted from an essay on "The Open Universities of South Africa" as follows: "There is no substitute for the clash of mind between colleague and colleague, between teacher and student, between student and student. . . . It is here the half-formed idea may take shape, the groundless belief be shattered, the developing theory be tested. . . . It is here the controversy develops, and out of controversy, deeper understanding." Today when there is doubt and skepticism concerning the very tradition of intellectual freedom and integrity upon which the intellectual pursuit of knowledge is based, it is important that the university through its faculty meet these questions head on.

This University has indeed been fortunate in the dedication which throughout the years it has evoked. It has been surrounded by a circle of friends, who by their aspirations for the university and their own self sacrifice have assured its pursuit of quality and its inner integrity.

I am proud to be in this place and I shall do my best.

Unrest and the Universities

Edward H. Levi

AN ADDRESS BY THE PRESIDENT OF THE UNIVERSITY
OF CHICAGO TO THE LIFE INSURANCE ASSOCIATION
OF AMERICA, NEW YORK CITY

DECEMBER 11, 1968

A month after his inaugural address, Edward Levi was invited to speak to an industry group that offered as guidance for his comments the relationship between widespread unrest in America's cities and the unrest prevailing on the nation's campuses. As in his inaugural address, Levi takes the long view, noting that unruly students have challenged universities throughout their history; misconduct is nothing new. "But the consolation of history does not work." Levi grants that dissatisfaction is a part of the abiding human condition—even something that should be "nurtured"—and that ideas "are properly subversive, frequently wrong." What is novel, for Levi, are fundamental changes in the relationship between universities and society. Thus, he understood the challenges that rose to the fore in his time as carrying specific, unique weight. His utmost concern pertaining to the pervasive unrest of late 1968 is what he sees as the decay in trust and regard for the legal system overall. There is only so much of such corrosion that a society can take before becoming fundamentally unstable. Politicization takes distinct forms in different eras, and Levi does not offer simple solutions. Instead, his address embodies a kind of Chicago virtue of clearly naming the problem of the moment. But it deserves noting that Levi's clarity is eerily prescient. We now face many of the trends he observed: weakening of the persuasive power of the law, an elevation of identity group interests to the point of eclipsing democratic cohesion, and, perhaps most of all, an eroded sense of common vision. The theme of common vision is one that Levi returns to, writing at one point that "we were told a long time ago that the penalty for no vision is severe," a likely reference to Proverbs 29:18.[1] This is an address of profound importance in our current era. While unrest and misconduct are clothed in new rhetorical fashions, the universal undercurrent continues to run through the life of the academy and the polis at a time in which the intensity of external forces and pressure on universities has only grown.

Your invitation asked me to explore with you a subject in the area of social unrest, keyed to the function of universities, but raising more general questions. As guidance, your Chairman referred to the connection between unrest in cities and that occurring on many campuses. I accept this guideline. Some aspects of university life are now high on the list for popular discussion. The described conduct appears to ask what kind of people we are or are becoming, what kind of society we have and what is to become of it? Unrest in the universities is trivialized if it is not seen in a larger and contemporary context.

Of course, there is another dimension. If unrest is taken as a euphemism for what is regarded at the time as misconduct, there has been plenty of it in universities from the beginning. The uproarious conduct of faculty and students, and town and gown disputes, closed medieval and renaissance universities and sometimes created new ones. In our own country Thomas Jefferson in 1823, thinking about his newly founded University of Virginia, said the rock he most dreaded was the discipline of the institution. "The insubordination of our youth[,]" he wrote[,] "is now the greatest obstacle to their education." He sought the advice of Professor Ticknor of Harvard on the handling of dissatisfaction, disobedience and revolt. Ticknor publicly had one bit of advice among others: "The longest vacation should happen in the hot season, when insubordination and misconduct are now most frequent." Fifty years later a prominent American professor of English, comparing German and American universities, thought it relevant to point out that the German professor's "temper is not ruffled by the freaks or down-right insults of mutinous youth."

When unrest centers around political issues of the society, we may console ourselves by remembering one tradition of thought which held it singly impossible to educate young people in such matters. "A young man," wrote Aristotle, "is not a proper hearer of lectures on political science, for he is inexperienced in the actions that occur in life . . . further since he tends to follow his passions, his study will be in vain and unprofitable because the end aimed at is not knowledge but action." Aristotle made it plain he was talking not only about the young in years but also about the "youthful in character." In his old age Plato had a number of solutions for the political propensities of the young. "Assuming you have reasonably good laws," he said, "one of the best of them will be the law forbidding any young man to enquire which of them are right or wrong; but with one mouth and one voice they must all agree the laws are all good." He thought an old man might criticize the laws, but only "when no young man is present."

But the consolation of history does not work. All crises of unrest speak to their own time. Ours speaks to us. It is a warning of failures, although perhaps not always the specific failures the dissidents have in mind. To say the manifestations of unrest have the significance of warnings, and thus have meaning, is not to characterize them, in one of the current platitudes, as simply another form of communication. That suggests the means chosen for the message are not as important as the reasons for dissatisfaction. But this is not necessarily true. We have to find out what is significant and important in both the means used and in the fact of dissatisfaction. This is not the same as looking for the causes or reasons for unrest. The human condition and aspirations being what they are, dissatisfaction is to be expected and nurtured. It is the particular form and manifestation which become important, as well as the failure of institutions of society to respond, guide or relate effectively to the force of discontent.

While I accept the significance of university discontent as a way of looking at problems of the society at large, this way of looking has its own distortion. The university has its closest relationship with a particular segment of the community, not only in part a population of the young, but also one which is more concerned with words and symbols. Universities are often regarded as mirrors for the larger society. Philosophers of social reconstruction frequently deny the power of their own thought to change the image, perhaps as a way of asserting the validity of their perception. So John Dewey, urging the social reconstruction of the nation in 1929, wrote, "Literary persons and academic thinkers are now more than ever, effects, not causes." But the interrelationship between the world of ideas and the facts of life is intricate. The university is or should be the home of ideas. Ideas are properly subversive, frequently wrong. They give power to see correctly and also, of course, to see incorrectly. On the level of ideas there is both a special responsiveness within the university community and also a stubborn selectivity. For related reasons there is vulnerability on the part of the university to certain forms of discontent. But these distortions help to magnify and thus to identify some of the problems of the society at large. They may help to identify our failures.

Our most pressing failure relates to our attitude toward the legal system. Civil disobedience and indifference to law have become sufficiently widespread to reflect and raise essentially naïve questions as to the function of law in a modern society. It is paradoxical that the civil rights movement which in the almost immediate past built upon the force of law, and depended so much on the morality of acquiescence, should now, to some extent, be the vehicle for the destruction of this acquiescence. The undeclared Viet Nam war has further emphasized the morality of illegal acts. It is, indeed, difficult to speak of the protest movements without appearing either to augment an alarmist view or to minimize or denegate their cause. The fact is they have occurred, and there are continuing consequences for the legal system. For some, these events have endorsed illegal protest as a way of life. Justification is felt or found in the sense of injustice, in history and in doctrine. So there is recollection of the illicit in the obdurate conflicts of the labor movement, or the compulsion of law is equated with colonialism. And there is excitement, the sense or fact of accomplishment which stands as a criticism of the lack of public goals within the life of conformity. One is reminded of the description of Britain at the time of the Suez crisis. "There was . . . a current wave of nostalgia for the last war, a sense of the boredom and fatuousness of contemporary Britain: it was the year of Look Back in Anger. . . . Nearly everyone seemed touchy, and when the Canal was seized there was an instinctive feeling that something must be done. There was a mood of almost tribal recidivism, like the moods that sweep through a school, which was not easy to resist."

But it is ancient wisdom that at some point violations of individual laws can greatly impair the shield necessary for the future welfare of the community. The burden upon the legal system has been substantial.

The fact is our legal system would have been in difficulty without this added burden. The increasing size of our communities are but one factor in making intolerable abuses or inadequacies which long ago should have been corrected. Consider a legal system which insists protest will be protected and need not cross the line of illegality, and yet compels the violation of law, with all the risks for the individual and the community which must accompany this, as the only road for testing the constitutionality of many statutes. Or a legal system which operates with a schedule of fines imposed without regard to the ability of the defendant to pay. Or a system which perpetually proclaims that justice delayed is justice denied, but accepts unconscionable delays, with the personal hardships this causes, as a necessary fact of life. Or a system which only in the last few years has moved to correct the vice of using poverty as a screen against the effective raising of defenses in criminal cases. These examples are perhaps not as important in themselves as they are tests of the sensitivity of the system to the kind of lesson it teaches. Viewing the legal system in its larger dimension, as one must, lessons are also taught by inadequate or abusive policing in urban areas, the misconduct of legislative committees, the passing of vindictive or unconstitutional laws, or the strange, sometimes called political, conduct of prosecuting attorneys.

It is inadequate to respond to this picture by saying it describes life in the United States which is, after all, pretty good. The description is of official action of the instruments of law. The operation of the legal system—for good or bad the greatest educational force in the society—inevitably creates a picture of the kind of community we would like to have. In this sense it either represents and speaks to our better selves or it carries a message of indifferent power or worse. The current unrest questions the persuasiveness of this system. Part of our difficulty perhaps arises as a concomitant of excessive reliance on judicial interpretation of the constitution. This may have weakened, as some have said it would, the thrust for legislative improvement of the system as a whole. Excessive reliance on changing constitutional doctrine creates other difficulties, increasing the sense of injustice by expectations which are then unfulfilled. The extension of constitutional doctrine sometimes carries a technical message where proper conduct and fairness should have been consciously resolved outside the courts as an issue of policy. But it is plainly wrong to blame the courts for what is chiefly the weakness of legislative and executive action. The problems of policy go beyond the structures we now have. We have to take account of the complexity of our cities and provide the forums, both judicial and legislative, perhaps places also for citizens' debate, which can win a personal response—a response upon which the magic of the legal system depends. In our own thinking we have to put civil rights and property rights together again. We need, in short, the organizing view of a jurisprudence.

This jurisprudence will have to speak to the current popular view of power and coercion. This is an extraordinary transformation of what was once accepted as the powers and responsibilities of citizens and officials in the American tradition. The transformation not only assumes, what some of us surely regard as quite false, that a necessary and desirable aim in life is power over others, but it sees coercion in all relationships, including the coercion of benefits. It then equates power with violence, assuming that violence within an established system is simply not separately recognized. What the conception does, in a fairly standard way, is to deny the legitimacy of governmental authority, or governmentally derived authority. It may or may not substitute some special human quality or condition as a substitute for that authority, and it may or may not impose some other restriction on violence. I mention this because this view, although perhaps not with all its implications, is furthered by a number of factors: the widespread use of the idea of the power structure itself; the undoubted influence of the manifestation of violence in international life coupled with the characterization of the United States as the primary power; the picture of government officials finding their fullest satisfaction in the manipulation of power; and the belief that in an affluent society choices are not severely limited by necessity. The view is also furthered by the assumption there are safeguards in the intention, motives or depth of feeling with which power is exercised. As I write these words I am haunted by an illustration used by Paul Tillich to describe the union of love and power. "We read that in the Middle Ages, during the trial and execution of a mass murderer," Tillich wrote, "the relatives of the murdered fell on their knees and prayed for his soul. The destruction of his bodily existence was not felt as a negation, but as an affirmation of love. It made the reunion of the radically separated soul of the criminal with himself and with the souls of his natural enemies possible." There is relatively little comfort in this dreadful tale.

The preoccupation with power and coercion undoubtedly reflects, as I have suggested, justified criticism of what appears to many as the central position given to power in our national vision. A society requires a vision of its better self. The legal system and other institutions serve to create it. One wonders what ours now is. We have not adjusted to the impact of new forms of communication or the intensity and immediacy with which all forms of communication can now operate. Our infirmities are there enlarged; our difficulties are endlessly and frequently erroneously explained. Yet what is portrayed, and even the arguments made, are not really strange to American history. Violence, the tension among groups, the domination by machines—these are themes ancient as our history runs. But something has happened to our understanding. It is, indeed, surprising that a society as much concerned with the crisis of identity of groups and of individuals should have failed to be more successfully introspective with regard to itself. It is this apparent lack of coming to terms with what we are which becomes the stated justification for confrontation. Yet we do recognize our current difficulties. What we fail to acknowledge or articulate is the imperfections and limitations in man himself—all men, young and old—imperfections which give rise to the necessity of living together in certain ways and under certain understandings. We have lost coherence and eloquence about our common condition, what is good that is here and in what we wish to become. It is not at all true that the way things are stated makes no difference. We have relied on forms of speech and perhaps of thought which are essentially degrading. Thus, one does not ask those who riot to cease doing so because they are chiefly hurting themselves and not others, or ask the community to do what it ought to do because if it does not there will be more riots and more destruction. This is not to assume that eloquence will carry its own implementation. But in fact it will help greatly. We have all been warned of the frustrations of promises, the awkward thud created by the dropping of goals stated in presidential task forces, the hollow ring of the promises of legislation. There is very little in these to win the commitment of a citizenry or to unify a society. The problem of the cities, of course, will remain. But one can evoke a difference—an approach more effective, more embracing. There is nothing which decrees that areas which need the most must be given. We are an idealistic people, and it is quite likely there will be a response. In any event, we were told a long time ago that the penalty for no vision is severe.

Disruption in the universities now reflects a weakening in the persuasive power of law. It reflects also an erosion of the discipline of the protest movements. The civil rights movement, when it created the climate of protest, for the most part made its case upon the lawfulness of its conduct. It was a step beyond, when conduct, with no serious claim to legality, was chosen to force confrontation. Yet even here civil disobedience required a special acquiescence in the idea of law. Civil disobedience, in terms of its own structure of justification, is a form of witnessing, an appeal to higher values, and it has required, as a confirmation of the nature of the act, that there be a willingness, indeed a desire, to accept the penalty for its violation of law. But this tradition has become ineffective as disruption itself becomes a primary aim and goal. This general or eclectic disruption is, apparently, to be taken as an attack upon society itself; a criticism through a kind of caricature of what is viewed as society's preoccupation with power and its manipulation; an imitation and adoption of the aggression which is protested. The references to particularly aggressive political figures of a past generation are frequent.

The universities are viewed as a part of the political society. They are regarded as an arm of the state because their work is important or necessary to the state's welfare. Moreover, the universities are thought to be used by the state to achieve the technological advances necessary for all kinds of power, including military; to feed the economy with trained persons, and also for the purpose of keeping young people out of the labor market. Whether the university is public or private—the argument goes on—it receives money from the federal government and, like everything else in our society, is affected with a public interest. Its claim to freedom is then regarded as an unfounded assertion of special privilege. Like all institutions and persons it is subject to coercion, and uses power—it is said. Thus the view is that it has coerced its students by attracting them with the benefit of essential training, and by being part of a society in which the selective service system puts pressure upon students to stay in school. It is, indeed, a community in which the student expects to spend many years. If he leaves, he will go to another one, said to be just like it, for, generally speaking, the rhetoric claims, the communities are interchangeable. Any argument that there are different kinds of institutions, and that the student voluntarily chose this one, is thought to forget the coercion he is said to be under, and in any event, is like telling a citizen of a country he can go to some other place. The institution's denial of certain kinds of power is then regarded as either hypocritical or an impossible attempt to abdicate responsibility, like the unconcerned citizen.

The central charge is that the institution is part of the political order and a proper target for politicizing. This view is furthered by politicians or statesmen who may not only view the universities much as the students do, but who also see the protesting as a kind of reflection—or at least so they hope—of their own interest. So the protests within educational institutions in Great Britain are translated by a member of the House of Commons into his own terms. He writes "Not all students I hope are content simply with a choice between Mr. Wilson and

Mr. Heath every five years. Not all students, as they contemplate an actual fall in the standard of living in this country and the appalling situation through famine in India or through war in Nigeria (where Socialist-capitalism is improving the balance of payments by selling arms), accept that British bureaucracy is the answer to the world's trouble. They believe they could do better." The revolt then can express a variety of dissatisfactions, avoiding the failure—and this is the illustration so frequently used—of the German professor to protest the rise of Hitler. As to this, Professor Dawson of Harvard has written: "Some memories are short. German universities in 1933 were occupied by storm troops, wearing brown shirts, not blue jeans. The German universities became instruments of political and social action and served their masters well." The Dawson argument would not be regarded as particularly cogent. It would be said that almost anyone should be able to distinguish good political ends from bad ones.

All this may well lead to the conclusion that it is good that disruption and unrest have found their way to colleges and universities because, after all, it is a problem for education. And yet for this very reason it is a peculiarly difficult problem for education to deal with. The movements tend to reject reason which is the way of education. They buttress this rejection by replacing reason with personal qualities thought to be more than adequate substitutes. As always, the corruptions of thought come home to roost. Moreover, coercion and disruption are, in fact, offensive to the very idea of a university. For this reason a university is most vulnerable to them. Over a long period of time it cannot live with them, and to the extent that they are present, they diminish and deteriorate the quality of the institution. And this comes at a time when the quality of intellectual life in our institutions is under attack in any event.

It is not certain there is an answer. But obviously the attempt has to be made. One would hope it can be most appropriately made through a patient reassertion of the universities' own conception of themselves as places for disciplined thought, as academies of the mind, as custodians of our culture, the restorers of eloquence, and the centers of that intellectual concern and unrest which can change the world.

Liberal Arts, Free Expression, and the Demosthenes-Feynman Trap

Robert J. Zimmer

REMARKS BY PRESIDENT ZIMMER UPON
RECEIVING THE 2017 PHILIP MERRILL AWARD

OCTOBER 20, 2017

Robert J. Zimmer will be remembered as one of the most influential University presidents of his era. Throughout his fifteen years in office, Zimmer displayed unfailing advocacy for free inquiry and expression. We have selected what we believe to be one of his stronger statements, a 2017 lecture given to the American Council of Trustees and Alumni (ACTA). ACTA honored Zimmer with its Philip Merrill Award for Outstanding Contributions to Liberal Arts Education, for which he wrote and delivered this piece, "Liberal Arts, Free Expression, and the Demosthenes-Feynman Trap." At the time, universities faced a cresting wave of cancel culture alongside declining ideological and viewpoint diversity. Zimmer, noting these dynamics soon after he took office in 2006, orchestrated the University's response by commissioning three of the faculty reports contained in this volume—including the one that has come to be known as the Chicago Principles. This address, however, goes deeper than the articulation of principles. Zimmer's concern here is the practice of free inquiry and expression, attuned to its ultimate purpose: a practice that to be developed must overcome the ubiquitous ease of self-deception. Each of us is prone to deluding ourselves, and this might even be positively correlated with intelligence. How, then, to escape its entrapment? Zimmer's argument shows that the ease of self-deception is overcome by wisdom, as distinct from intelligence, and evident in two scholarly examples, millennia apart. Richard Feynman, a Nobel laureate theoretical physicist, returns to the wisdom of the ancients by echoing Demosthenes: "The first principle is that you must not fool yourself—and you are the easiest person to fool." The elegance of this paradoxically simple argument has withstood the test of time, and it has an important corollary: to overcome the delusions of confirmation bias, a community of discursive partners is an absolute necessity. It is only such good faith interlocutors who can see the blind spots and deceptions that cast their shadows over each individual mind. Scholarship, wisdom, discovery, and knowledge thrive in such settings, the maintenance of which is the imperative of excellent colleges and universities, steadfast in their commitment to free expression and open inquiry.

Almost 2400 years ago, the great Athenian orator Demosthenes wrote: "The wish is parent to the thought, and that is why nothing is easier than self-deceit. For what each person wishes, that they also believe to be true." Demosthenes was not talking about deceiving ourselves on a personal level, but rather in our views of the world at large.

The phenomenon identified by Demosthenes has remained with us over the millennia. Speaking of science in the broadest possible sense, the great American physicist Richard Feynman said during his Caltech commencement address in 1974: "The first principle is that you must not fool yourself—and you are the easiest person to fool."

Both Demosthenes and Feynman use the same word—easy—to describe the tendency to self-deceit, and the word "easy" is important to emphasize. It is not just that fooling oneself is common, it is the easy and in that sense natural state of humankind. A physicist might describe this as the lowest energy state, which means that energy must be applied to be in a different situation. Moving beyond it will not happen automatically. Without effort, often purposeful effort, we are all caught in this Demosthenes-Feynman trap.

Liberal arts education, at its best, provides such an effort. Learning to recognize and challenge one's own and others' assumptions, the confrontation of new and different ideas, understanding the power and limitations of an argument, perceiving the importance of context, history, and culture, understanding the ubiquity of complexity, recognizing when to forgo the temptation of simplicity, grappling with exposure to unfamiliar modes of inquiry, synthesizing different perspectives, and being able to articulately and coherently advocate a position—all these are skills that students should acquire through their education and that faculty need to impart in delivering that education. Central to this education are free expression, open discourse, rigorous argument, diverse perspectives being brought forth by individuals with different backgrounds and experiences, freedom to express views that may be unpopular or contrary to any consensus, and the multiple intellectual challenges these activities generate. It is an education designed to teach students to think critically in multiple ways, and designed to impart a set of lifelong habits of mind and intellectual skills. These are indeed liberal arts, or in other words liberating skills, that enable us, at least to some extent, to free ourselves from the Demosthenes-Feynman trap of self-deception in thought.

One often hears liberal arts education described as being valuable for personal development while being dismissed as impractical. In fact, this is a traditional view of the liberal arts going back many centuries, and a number of proponents of liberal arts education today are comfortable with this view. However, while the value for personal development is surely accurate, the assertion of impracticality is not. The habits of mind and intellectual skills of questioning and challenge that are gained from the demanding form of liberal arts education I have just described are a powerful and even necessary tool in many areas, particularly for leadership in an environment of complexity. Such leaders are inevitably faced with integrating different perspectives, understanding context and uncertainty, and questioning both power and limitations in a wide variety of arguments, approaches, and options. Getting out of the Demosthenes-Feynman trap is critical to being effective—leadership governed by self-deceit cannot be so. In this light, a high quality liberal arts education is in fact an excellent training ground for students who will soon be entering the world of work.

A concrete example is illuminating. Climate change is a question that is confronted in various ways by leaders around the world in government, business, science, technology, education, and non-profits. In order to understand this issue both seriously and broadly, here are some higher order questions that arise independent of one's viewpoint on climate change. What is the nature of scientific evidence and conclusion? How do you understand uncertainty? How does one think about risk? What forms of government are capable of making, executing, and sustaining what types of decisions? What type of trade-offs are different countries able or willing to make and why? How does technological change happen? How do societal culture and history affect market behavior, policy choices and outcomes? When can nations act collectively and when can they not? What approach can one take to analyze the impact of law and regulation?

These are the types of questions one learns to confront in a quality liberal arts education. They are all questions that many people, including some with strong views on climate change, will either never consider or respond to with unexamined and even unrecognized assumptions. Each question by itself does not give a full perspective on climate change, but each is necessary to gain a sophisticated perspective on climate change. There are no "final" answers to any of these questions. Independent of particular conclusions or viewpoints, leaders needing to confront this issue will have limited likelihood of success if they remain in the Demosthenes-Feynman trap.

I have spoken of quality liberal arts education as both personally expanding and empowering in work. Yet, liberal arts education is under serious threat in the United States today. As we are all aware, there is a major assault on free expression and open discourse taking place on many campuses across the country. Many universities and colleges confront demands made by groups of students and some faculty that speakers with certain views (always views they disagree with) be prevented from speaking, and that universities adopt policies that limit the ideas faculty, students, and visitors should be allowed to present or hear. Others confront similar demands made by persons outside the university. As I have indicated, free expression, open discourse, rigorous argumentation, and freedom to express unpopular views lie at the very core of a liberal arts education. To diminish free expression is quite simply to diminish the quality of education. It is imperative for those of us responsible for high quality education to reaffirm this value and to resist these efforts to suppress speech. As we all recognize, the response of faculty and university leaders across the country has been uneven.

I am going to discuss three related but distinct aspects of the current threat to free expression.

First is what one might call the "no discomfort" argument. One of the persistent rationales for demands emanating from students and sometimes faculty to suppress speech is concern about discomfort. If students feel uncomfortable, this argument goes, there is something amiss and discourse needs to be controlled to correct it. Many of the persons who make this argument are of good will and are projecting empathy for those who might feel uncomfortable by the expression of certain views. Many students come out of a high school environment in which this perspective is forcefully articulated, sometimes as one of the highest values of that educational environment.

One of the benefits of seeing education through the lens of the Demosthenes-Feynman trap is that it highlights how deeply misguided this argument is. Because education can help liberate us from the Demosthenes-Feynman trap, and because this trap is defined by an easy and comfortable state, it follows that an effective education is in fact intrinsically uncomfortable at times. Without discomfort and the challenge that stimulates it, there is no escape for thought being submerged by an ongoing state of self-deception. The argument for avoiding discomfort, therefore, is an argument against liberal arts education itself and against the empowerment that such education brings. Those who argue for avoiding discomfort, while seemingly seeking to aid students, are in fact doing all students a great disservice—they are advocating for reducing the quality of education, and along with it the capacity of students to apply critical and independent thought to the world.

One of the drivers for the prevalence of the no discomfort argument that we often hear today is exclusionary behavior. There is no question that there is a powerful history of exclusionary behavior in this society, as in all societies. Our history is replete with slavery, racism, misogyny, homophobia, and discrimination against religious and ethnic groups. Universities should all be striving to confront the continuing impact of these forces, and there is no question that creating an inclusive and respectful campus community requires serious and sustained work and attention. This effort is needed to ensure that all students feel sufficiently empowered to participate in the university's intellectual discourse. But part of that empowerment is helping students to accept the discomfort caused by conflicting views, and to see it as an intrinsic part of their own education and advancement. Automatically viewing discomfort caused by free expression and open discourse as problematic has the ironic result of establishing a new type of exclusionary behavior—excluding students from the best and most challenging education that universities can provide.

Another feature of the "no discomfort" argument is an unfortunate and naïve neglect, and perhaps ignorance, of history. It is dangerous for a group with one particular perspective to advocate for special exceptions to a commitment to free and open expression. If universities allow some views to be suppressed, it is certain that other views, not always concordant views, will be suppressed over time. If those who were certain they were right were empowered to silence those whose views made them "uncomfortable," we would never have had a civil rights, women's rights, or gay rights movement on our campuses or in our nation.

A second aspect of the threat to free expression and the liberal arts education it supports is an attack on the very core of the university's role in society, an attack seeking to turn universities into a political or moral battleground. While the "no discomfort" argument generally comes from within the university, this second threat, not benign in intent, comes from both within and outside the university.

Universities' openness to divergent and clashing ideas, to analytic debate, to rigor, and to questioning, is a critical ingredient in illuminating societal, scientific, and humanistic issues. The greatest contributions universities can make to society over the long run are the ideas and discoveries of faculty and students that emanate from the intellectual ferment of such a challenging environment and the work of alumni across the scope of human endeavor empowered by their education. That universities are virtually unique in making this long-term contribution only highlights their importance to society.

The openness of universities, and therefore their most fundamental value to society, is under threat by those who view the university as a political or moral battleground and seek to impose their own views on others by suppressing speech, sometimes being willing to use disruption and even violence to do so. We have seen many such examples in recent years. Such groups, independent of their particular views, claim moral superiority and act with an urgency driven by self-righteousness. The suppression of speech and open discourse by disruption or violence has been present with us through the millennia, and such conduct today only adds to this problematic history. One wonders when the logic of preventing someone from speaking and others from listening translates into preventing the library from having certain books. It is not that great a leap. We need to recognize very clearly, whether these groups come from within or outside the university and without regard to their political or moral view, that they stand fundamentally opposed to the foundations of what a university is, the nature of its societal contributions, and what an education should be.

A third aspect of the threat to free expression and liberal arts education is the role of university and college faculty and leaders. Each institution needs to decide what it is and what it stands for. Faculty, deans, provosts, and presidents, as well as trustees, individually and together, have a fundamental role in defining institutional values and how they are realized. Institutions may not all come to the same conclusion. But clarity about what an institution's values are and the expression of these values is important to each.

Many faculty and institutional leaders see themselves in a complex position with respect to free expression. They deal with complicated constituencies, multiple pressures and responsibilities, and competition for their time and attention. Many are now working on campuses in which free expression, even as an ideal, has been eroded. Some faculty and university leaders have strong political views themselves. The "no discomfort" argument, misguided as it is, can be seen by some as having a moral high ground based on the perception of empathy. Particularly in situations in which free expression is already eroded, a path to reversing the trend may not be straightforward.

We see here another potential Demosthenes-Feynman trap. Namely, will some university faculty and leaders think the erosion of free expression and the concomitant diminution of the quality of liberal arts education are acceptable? Will they deceive themselves in thinking this erosion is not profoundly damaging either because they are sympathetic to a particular set of political views or because such an approach makes life easier for them in the short run? Are some university faculty and leaders caught in their own version of the Demosthenes-Feynman trap around this critical issue?

The saddest and most troubling development would be that faculty members and academic leaders, all of whom have the obligation to deliver outstanding education, become comfortable with the erosion of free expression, and relegate it to just one of the many things they deal with rather than supporting it as fundamental to education. To do so would be to fall into the very Demosthenes-Feynman trap that liberal arts education is designed to confront. This third aspect of the threat to free expression, namely that faculty and academic leaders may not escape the Demosthenes-Feynman trap of comfort with the erosion of free expression and of liberal arts education, may be the greatest long-term threat of all.

Let me conclude on a positive note. Just fifteen months ago, it was almost unheard of for open discussion of these issues to be taking place on most university and college campuses. The visible silence on the issue was itself a reflection of the erosion of free expression and open discourse. Within the past year, a number of university leaders and faculty have argued forcefully for the importance of free expression, and I for one am deeply appreciative of their actions. I am pleased that the Chicago Principles, reflecting the long-standing commitment of the University of Chicago, its faculty, and its leaders to free expression, have been a useful stimulus and tool in the emerging national discussion and have provided a model for a number of university faculty and leaders around the country to take a strong stand in support of free expression.

As educators, we have a collective obligation to give all our students the most enriching and empowering education we can. To this end, supporting open discourse and free expression is not a task we can take lightly. We cannot view its erosion with comfort or complacency, and we should not deceive ourselves in thinking this erosion is not profoundly damaging. For the sake of today's students and those who will follow them, we must reaffirm our commitment to the spirit of the liberating skills, to the liberal arts, and to the free and open discourse and questioning that lie at their core.

excerpts from aims of education addresses

Free Speech on Campus

A CHALLENGE OF OUR TIMES

Geoffrey R. Stone

SEPTEMBER 22, 2016

Geoffrey R. Stone is the Edward H. Levi Distinguished Service Professor at the University of Chicago. Mr. Stone joined the faculty in 1973, after serving as a law clerk to Supreme Court Justice William J. Brennan Jr. He later served as dean of the Law School (1987–1994) and provost of the University of Chicago (1994–2002). Professor Stone is the author of many books on constitutional law, including *Perilous Times: Free Speech in Wartime from the Sedition Act of 1798 to the War on Terrorism* (2004). He chaired the Committee on Freedom of Expression appointed by President Zimmer in 2014.

. . . I should like to begin by telling you a bit about my world. It is the world of the law. More specifically, it is the world of constitutional law. Law is about stories. It is about real people involved in real disputes with real consequences. So, I shall tell you a story.

This story begins during World War I. As you may or may not know, World War I was not a particularly popular war with the American people, whose sympathies were divided. Many Americans vigorously opposed the Wilson administration's decision to intervene in the conflict that was then raging in Europe, arguing that our intervention was both unwise and immoral.

Not surprisingly, such opposition did not sit well with the government. In 1917 Attorney General Thomas Gregory, attacking the loyalty of war opponents, declared: "May God have mercy on them, for they can expect none from . . . an avenging government."

Gregory wasn't kidding about the "avenging" government. In 1918, Congress enacted the Sedition Act, which made it a crime for any person to utter "any disloyal, . . . scurrilous, or abusive language intended to cause contempt . . . for the . . . government of the United States, the Constitution, or the flag." True to the Attorney General's threat, federal authorities launched more than 2,000 prosecutions against individuals who wrote or spoke against the war or the draft.

One such prosecution involved five young, Russian-Jewish emigrants who were roughly your age at the time. In the summer of 1918, the United States sent a contingent of marines to Vladivostok in Russia. Concerned that this was the first step of an American effort to crush the Russian Revolution, these five self-proclaimed socialists threw several thousand copies of each of two leaflets—one in English, the other in Yiddish—from several rooftops on the lower east side of New York City.

The leaflets, which were boldly signed "The Rebels," were addressed to other Russian emigrants. After stating that the Rebels hated "German militarism," they warned those who worked in ammunition factories that they were "producing bullets, bayonets and cannon to murder not only the Germans, but also your dearest, your best, who are in Russia and are fighting for their freedom."

The "Rebels" were immediately arrested by the military police. After a controversial trial, they were convicted of violating the Sedition Act of 1918. The trial judge, disgusted by their behavior and their beliefs, sentenced the Rebels to terms ranging up to twenty years in prison.

The Rebels appealed their convictions to the Supreme Court of the United States, claiming that their convictions violated the First Amendment, which guarantees that "Congress shall make no law . . . abridging the freedom of speech." In *Abrams v. United States*, the Supreme Court, in a seven-to-two decision, rejected this claim and upheld the convictions. For the majority of the Court, this was an easy case. Because the natural tendency of the defendants' speech was to generate opposition to the war, it was not within "the freedom of speech" protected by the Constitution.

Justice Oliver Wendell Holmes, the same Justice Holmes who some years later was to lose his railway ticket, dissented. Holmes's dissenting opinion in *Abrams* is worth reading, for it remains one of the most eloquent statements ever written by a Justice of the Supreme Court about the freedom of expression.

Holmes wrote:

> Persecution for the expression of opinion seems to me perfectly logical. If you have no doubt of your premises . . . and want a certain result with all your heart you naturally [want to] sweep away all opposition. . . . But when men have realized that time has upset many fighting faiths, they may come to believe . . . that the ultimate good desired is better reached by free trade in ideas—that the best test of truth is the power of the thought to get itself accepted in the competition of the market, and that truth is the only ground upon which their wishes safely can be carried out.

Holmes therefore concluded that "we should be eternally vigilant against attempts to check the expression" even of "opinions that we loathe and believe to be fraught with death, unless they so imminently threaten" compelling government interests that an immediate check is necessary to save the nation.

I first read this passage, written almost a century ago, when I was a law student at this University, almost half-a-century ago. It has engaged my energy and curiosity ever since. Indeed, I think it's fair to say that it was my puzzling over this passage under the probing tutelage of my law school professor Harry Kalven that, for better or worse, put me on the path to my career and, indeed, to where I stand before you this evening.

But now I must change direction, for this is not to be a discourse on the First Amendment. It is, rather, to be a talk about the aims of education. Happily, these are not unrelated subjects. To the contrary, the longer I have puzzled over the meaning of free expression, and the longer I have thought about education, the more the two seem to me to converge. Indeed, neither really is worth all that much without the other. And, with that in mind, I would like to turn to what I see as the intersection of free expression and education, and to the subject of academic freedom, for it is at this intersection that we will find the most fundamental values of the world you are about to enter.

I hope to accomplish three things in this part of my talk. First, I will trace briefly for you the history of academic freedom, for it is only by understanding where we have been that we can appreciate—in both senses of the word—where we are today. Second, I will talk a bit about *this* University and about the special role it has played in the struggle to establish and to preserve academic freedom. And third, I will offer some thoughts about what this all means for you and about the responsibilities that we today bear in common.

It is important to understand that, like the freedom of speech, academic freedom is not a law of nature. It does not exist of its own force. It is always vulnerable, and should never be taken for granted. Indeed, until well into the nineteenth century, real freedom of thought was neither practiced nor professed in American universities.

To the contrary, any real freedom of inquiry or expression in American colleges in this era was smothered by the dominance of religion and by the prevailing theory of "doctrinal moralism," which assumed that the worth of an idea must be judged by what the institution's leaders declared its moral value to be. Thus, through the first half of the nineteenth century American colleges squelched any notion of free and open discussion or intellectual curiosity. Any student or faculty member who dared argue, for example, that women were equal to men, that blacks were equal to whites, or that homosexuality was not immoral would surely be expelled or fired without hesitation.

Similarly, through the first half of the nineteenth century, as the nation moved towards Civil War, any professor or student in the North who openly defended slavery, or any professor or student in the South who openly challenged slavery, could readily be dismissed, disciplined, or expelled. When a professor at the University of North Carolina expressed sympathy for the 1856 Republican presidential candidate, the students burned him in effigy and he was dismissed by the trustees. When a professor at Franklin College in Pennsylvania admitted he was not an abolitionist, he was promptly fired.

Several decades later, a furious battle arose over Charles Darwin's theory of evolution, with traditionalists charging not only that Darwin was wrong, but also that his beliefs were dangerous, immoral, and ungodly. As a consequence of the furious battle in the academy over evolution, new academic goals came to be embraced.

For the first time, to criticize, as well as to preserve, traditional moral values and understandings became an accepted function of higher education, and by 1892 William Rainey Harper, the first president of the University of Chicago, could boldly assert: "When for any reason the administration of a university attempts to dislodge a professor or punish a student because of his political or religious sentiments, at that moment the institution has ceased to be a university."

But despite such noble sentiments, the battle for academic freedom has been a continuing and fiercely contentious one. In the closing years of the nineteenth century, for example, businessmen who had accumulated vast industrial wealth began to support universities on an unprecedented scale. But that support was not without strings, and during this era professors who offended wealthy donors by criticizing their business practices were dismissed from such leading universities as Cornell and Stanford.

Then, during the World War I, patriotic zealots persecuted and, as we have seen, even prosecuted those who questioned the wisdom or morality of the war. In the face of such outrage, universities collapsed almost completely in their defense of academic freedom. Students and professors were systematically expelled and fired at colleges and universities across the nation merely for encouraging a spirit of indifference toward the war.

Similar issues arose again, with a vengeance, during the Cold War in the age of Joseph McCarthy. In the late 1940s and 1950s, most universities excluded those even suspected of Communist sympathies from university life. Yale President Charles Seymour, for example, went so far as to boast that "there will be no witch hunts at Yale, because there will be no witches. We will neither admit nor hire anyone with Communist sympathies."

As this history demonstrates, the freedom to question, the freedom to challenge, the freedom to inquire is not to be taken for granted. Academic freedom is, in fact, a hard-bought acquisition in an endless struggle to preserve the right of each individual, student and faculty alike, to seek wisdom, knowledge, and truth, free of the censor's sword.

But what does all of this have to do with you and with the University of Chicago? Well, from its very founding, the University of Chicago has been at the forefront of the struggle to define and to preserve academic freedom.

At the turn of the twentieth century, when universities across the land faced bitter conflicts between their trustees and their professors, President William Rainey Harper emphasized that: "Whatever may or may not have happened in other universities, in the University of Chicago neither the Trustees, nor the President, nor anyone in official position [may call] an instructor to account for any public utterances." "A donor," Harper added, "has the privilege of ceasing to make his gift . . . but . . . he has no right to interfere with . . . the instruction of the university."

Then, in the 1930s, a student organization invited Communist leader William Z. Foster to campus to discuss his perspectives on American society. This invitation triggered furious demands that the University should withdraw the invitation and punish the students for their audacity. In the face of those demands, University of Chicago President Robert Maynard Hutchins fearlessly backed our students, insisting that, at this institution, "students . . . have the freedom to discuss any problem that presents itself." Echoing Justice Holmes in *Abrams*, Hutchins declared that the only proper response even to ideas that we hate "lies through open discussion" and debate, rather "than through inhibition."

Fifteen years later, our University confronted another direct threat to its academic integrity. It was the age of Joseph McCarthy, and in the spring of 1949 the infamous "Broyles Bills" were introduced in the Illinois legislature. These bills prohibited any person who was "directly or indirectly affiliated with any communist . . . organization" to hold any governmental position in the State of Illinois.

A group of 106 intrepid University of Chicago students traveled to the state capital to oppose this legislation. The Illinois legislators were furious. One proclaimed that he would not send his "pet dog to the University of Chicago" and another asserted that "the students looked so dirty and greasy on the outside that they couldn't possibly be clean American on the inside."

In the wake of these protests, Senator Broyles launched a formal investigation of the University of Chicago to determine whether the University harbored professors who were indoctrinating students with subversive and "un-American" beliefs. President Robert Maynard Hutchins was the first witness to testify before the Broyles Committee. Listen to what Hutchins had to say:

"[Our] students . . . were entirely right to disapprove of [the] pending legislation. . . . It is now fashionable to call anybody with whom we disagree a Communist. . . . One who thinks that there are too many slums and too much lynching in America can be called a [Communist], for the Russians say the same . . .

"[As] is well known," Hutchins added, "there is a Communist Club among the students of the University. [Its] members . . . are interested in studying Communism, and some of them, perhaps all of them, may be sympathetic towards Communism. . . .

"[The] policy of the University [of Chicago] is to permit students to band together for any lawful purpose in terms of their common interests. . . . The University [asserts] that the policy of education is better than the policy of repression. . . ."

At the conclusion of the hearings, a petition bearing the names of 3,000 courageous University of Chicago students was submitted to the investigative committee. The petition read:

As students of the University of Chicago, we believe that the position of our University, which encourages and maintains the free examination of all ideas, is the strongest possible safeguard against indoctrination. . . . Because we believe that the policy of academic freedom for both students and teachers is the best preparation for effective citizenship in the American tradition, we are confident that the people in the State and nation will join with us to encourage the freedom of the University of Chicago and to support it against attack.

I say these students were "courageous" because, in the perilous days in which they lived, they were taking a serious risk in putting their names on so "subversive" a statement. In the era of the blacklist, they were placing their careers and their futures on the line. They made our University proud, and they make us proud to this day.

What Hutchins and our students stood up for was the central principle of free expression and free inquiry, a principle that invites bold challenge, controversy, and argument, a principle that, as Dean John Boyer has written, was "one of the foundational ideals on which this University was established." It is, indeed, at the very core of who we are.

Two decades after the Broyles incident, in the 1960s, the University of Chicago, like other universities, found itself buffeted by the storms of the Vietnam War. The University appointed a committee, chaired appropriately by Harry Kalven, the professor who taught me about the freedom of expression, to advise the University about its appropriate role in this conflict.

The Kalven Report boldly declared: "A university faithful to its mission will provide enduring challenges to social values, policies, practices, and institutions. . . . To perform [this mission], a university must sustain an extraordinary environment of freedom of inquiry, [and must] embrace, be hospitable to, and encourage the widest diversity of views."

How, though, do we sustain such an environment of free inquiry? First, like the students of 1949, we must defend academic freedom when it comes under attack. Like every liberty that is precious to us, the preservation of academic freedom demands vigilance, determination and, sometimes, courage.

Second, we must struggle to define the meaning of academic freedom in our time. As we saw in *Abrams*, the Constitution's guarantee of freedom of speech is not self-defining. Neither is academic freedom.

Each generation must give life to this concept in the face of the distinctive conflicts that arise over time.

Today, the principal challenge to academic freedom comes not from outside the academy, but from within it—from students themselves, some of whom demand censorship of ideas that they find distasteful, and from faculty members and college and university administrators who, afraid to offend their own students, too often surrender academic freedom to charges of offense.

To give just a few examples, several colleges and universities, including Brown, Johns Hopkins, and Williams, have recently withdrawn speaker invitations because of student objections to the views of the invited speakers.

Northwestern University recently subjected a professor to a sustained sexual harassment investigation for publishing an essay in the *Chronicle of Higher Education* that criticized Northwestern's sexual harassment investigations.

Colorado College suspended a student for making a joke that mocked feminism, William & Mary disciplined students for criticizing its affirmative action program, and the University of Kansas disciplined a professor for condemning the National Rifle Association.

At Wesleyan University, after the school newspaper published a student op-ed criticizing the Black Lives Matter movement, other students demanded that the University defund the school paper, at Amherst College, students demanded that the administration remove posters stating that "All Lives Matter," at Emory University, students demanded that the university punish other students who had chalked "Trump in 2016" on the university's sidewalks because, in their words, a university is "supposed to be a safe place and this made us feel unsafe, at DePaul University students shouted down a speaker whose views they opposed, causing the event to be cancelled, and a tenured professor at LSU was fired after students complained that she used profanity in class.

To put all this in perspective, a recent survey revealed that 72 percent of college students today support disciplinary action against any student or faculty member who expresses views that they deem to be "racist, sexist, homophobic or otherwise offensive."

So, where did all this come from? It was not too long ago when students were demanding the right to free speech. Now, at least some students demand the right to be free from speech that they find to be offensive, upsetting, or emotionally disturbing. What explains this profound shift in attitude?

One often-expressed theory is that at least some members of this generation of students have been raised by so-called helicopter parents who protected and celebrated them in every way, shielding them at every turn from the risks of failure, frustration, and defeat. On this theory, these students, unlike their predecessors, have never learned to deal effectively with challenge, uncertainty, insult, or fear. They therefore demand the right to be protected from speech that they find to be offensive, hurtful, or demeaning.

Another possible explanation of the current situation is that this generation of students is more attuned than their predecessors to the injustices of society, to the harmful impact of hateful expression, and to the inequalities that poison our nation. On this view of the matter, students today are not timid, but bold. They seek not shelter, but justice.

Still another possible explanation is that some students, particularly those who come from disadvantaged, marginalized, and discriminated against backgrounds, have always felt unwelcome on college campuses, but in the past they simply remained silent. On this view of the matter, this generation of college students, particularly those who themselves feel unwelcome and alienate, deserves credit, because instead of remaining silent in the face of oppression, they have the courage to demand equality and respect.

My own view, for what it's worth, is that there is an element of truth in all of these perspectives. The question is what to do about all this.

Faced with the ongoing challenge to academic freedom at American universities, in 2014 University of Chicago President Robert Zimmer charged a faculty committee with the task of drafting a formal statement for the University on Freedom of Expression. The goal of that committee, which I chaired, was to stake out *our* University's position on these issues. The committee consisted of seven distinguished faculty members from across the University. After broad consultation, we produced a brief, three-page Report.

At the risk of being self-indulgent, I want to read you some excerpts from that Report:

> Because the University [of Chicago] is committed to free and open inquiry in all matters, it guarantees all members of the University community the broadest possible latitude to speak, write, listen, challenge, and learn.
>
> In a word, the University's fundamental commitment is to the principle that robust debate and deliberation may not be suppressed because the ideas put forth are thought by some or even by most members of the University community to be offensive, unwise, immoral, or wrong-headed.
>
> It is for the individual members of the community, not for the University as an institution, to make those judgments for themselves, and to act on those judgments not by seeking to suppress speech, but by openly and vigorously contesting the ideas that they oppose.
>
> Indeed, fostering the ability of members of the University community to engage in such debate and deliberation in an effective and responsible manner is an essential part of the University's educational mission.
>
> As a corollary to the University's commitment to protect and promote free expression, members of the University community must also act in conformity with the principle of free expression.
>
> Although members of the University are free to criticize and contest the views expressed on campus, and although they are free to criticize and contest speakers who are invited to express their views on campus, they may not obstruct or otherwise interfere with the freedom of others to express views they reject or even loathe.
>
> To this end, the University has a solemn responsibility not only to promote a lively and fearless freedom of debate and deliberation, but also to protect that freedom when others attempt to restrict it. . . .

Interestingly, when we wrote this Report, we were thinking only about the University of Chicago. To our surprise, the Report has had a national and even international impact. Not only has it been lauded by editorials in such journals as the *New York Times*, the *Washington Post*, and the *Wall Street Journal*, but it has now been adopted by a range of other colleges and universities, including such diverse institutions as Princeton, Columbia, the University of Minnesota, the University of Missouri, Purdue, Johns Hopkins, American University, and the University of Wisconsin.

Now that I've finished congratulating myself, let me elaborate a bit. Why should a university take the position that faculty and students should be free to advance any and all ideas, however offensive, obnoxious, and wrong-headed they might be?

First, one thing we have learned from bitter experience is that even the ideas we hold to be most certain might in fact turn out to be wrong. As confident as we might be in our own wisdom, experience teaches that certainty is different from truth. If those who believed with absolute certainty that the earth was the center of the universe were wrong, if those who believed with absolute certainty in creationism were wrong, if those who believed that slavery was natural, right, and proper were wrong, if those who believed that a woman's place is in the home were wrong, then why should we have the arrogance to think that we are unquestionably right about our own beliefs today? The only wise approach, as Justice Holmes made clear, is to acknowledge the risk that our certainties might be wrong as well, and that they too must always be open to challenge and question.

Second, experience teaches that the suppression of speech breeds the suppression of speech. If today I am permitted to silence those whose views I find distasteful, I have then opened the door to allow others down the road to silence me. The neutral principle of no suppression of ideas protects us all. This is especially important in the current situation, for in the long run it is likely to be minorities, whether religious minorities, racial minorities, or political minorities, who are most likely to be silenced once censorship is deemed acceptable. Censorship is never a one-way street, and this is a door we do not want to open.

Third, a central precept of free expression is the concern with chilling effect. That problem is especially acute today because of the effects of social media. It used to be the case that students and faculty members were willing to take controversial positions, in part because the risks were relatively modest. One could say something provocative or outrageous, and the statement soon disappeared from view. But in a world of social media, where every comment you make can be circulated to the world and can be called up later by prospective employers or graduate schools or neighbors with the mere click of a button, the potential cost of speaking courageously—of taking controversial positions, of taking risks—is greater than ever before in history. Indeed, according to a recent survey, 65 percent of all college students now say that it is "unsafe" for them to express unpopular views, and this clearly has had an effect on faculty as well. In this setting, it is especially important for universities to stand up for free expression.

So, how should this work in practice? Should students be allowed to express whatever views they want—however offensive they might be to others? Yes. Absolutely.

Should those who disagree and are offended by the views and speech of others be allowed to condemn those views and speakers in the most vehement terms? Yes. Absolutely.

Should students, faculty, and community members who oppose a speaker be permitted to disrupt an event in order to prevent that individual from speaking? Absolutely not.

Should those who are offended and who disagree be allowed to demand that the university punish those who have offended them? Yes. Absolutely.

Should the university punish those whose speech annoys, offends, and insults others? Absolutely not.

Should students, faculty members and community members who oppose a speaker disrupt an event in order to prevent that individual from speaking? Absolutely not. Although non-disruptive protests are both permitted and encouraged, disruption of the rights of others to speak and to listen is wholly incompatible with the central principle of academic freedom.

Does this mean that the University may never restrict speech? No, as our committee noted in the University Statement on Free Expression, the University may restrict expression that violates the law, that falsely defames a specific individual, that constitutes a genuine threat or harassment, that unjustifiably invades substantial privacy or confidentiality interests, or that is otherwise directly incompatible with the core functioning of the University. But these are narrow exceptions to the general principle of freedom of expression, and it is vitally important that these exceptions never be used in a manner that is inconsistent with the University's commitment to a completely free and open discussion of ideas.

What, though, *should* a university do? First, a university should educate its students and faculty about the importance of a civility and mutual respect. As a member of the Class of '67 recently wrote to me, a university "has an obligation to create a community of people as well as 'a community of ideas,' a place where everyone feels certain that they are unambiguously welcomed." This is, indeed, a core institutional value, and it is one to which the University of Chicago is deeply committed. But it is a value that should be reinforced and reaffirmed by education and example, not by censorship.

Second, a university should encourage free, open, and robust disagreement, argument, and debate. It should instill in its students and faculty the importance of winning the day by facts, by ideas, and by persuasion, rather than by force, disruption, or censorship. Indeed, for a university to fulfill its most fundamental mission, for a university to be a university, it must be a safe space for even the most loathsome, offensive, and disloyal arguments. As a former member of the Law School faculty, who just happens now to be President of the United States, observed in a recent commencement address: No matter "how much you might disagree" with a speaker, don't try "to shut them down. . . ." Let them talk, but "have the confidence to challenge them." "If the other side has a point, learn from them. If they're wrong, rebut them. . . . Beat them on the battlefield of ideas. And you might as well start practicing now, because one thing I can guarantee you—you will have to deal with ignorance, hatred, racism" and stupidity "at every stage of your life."

Third, a university must recognize that, our society being flawed as it is, the costs of free speech will often fall most heavily on those groups and individuals who feel the most marginalized, unwelcome, and disrespected. All of us feel that way sometimes, but in our often unjust society the individuals who most often bear the brunt of free speech—or at least of certain types of free speech—tend to be racial and ethnic minorities; religious minorities; women; gays, lesbians, and transsexuals; immigrants; ideological dissidents; and the like. Universities must be sensitive to this reality. Even if they cannot "solve" this problem by censorship, they can and should take other steps to address the special challenges faced by groups and individuals who are most often made to feel unwelcome and unvalued by others.

Universities must take this challenge seriously. They should encourage civility and mutual respect. They should support students who feel vulnerable, marginalized, silenced, and demeaned. They should help those students learn how to speak up, how to respond effectively, how to challenge those whose attitudes, whose words, and whose beliefs offend, appall, and outrage them. This is a core responsibility of universities, for the world is not a safe space, and it is our job to enable our graduates to win the battles they will need to fight in the years and decades to come. This is not a challenge that universities can or should ignore.

As you no doubt are aware, the letter you received last month from Dean of Students Jay Ellison generated a good deal of attention about trigger warnings and safe spaces, so let me say a word about those issues. A trigger warning is an oral or written statement by a professor alerting students that material in a course might be upsetting to some students because of their backgrounds or their personal experiences. Examples might be material that includes graphic depictions of rape, of lynchings, or of the Holocaust. The idea is that students who might be especially distraught by such material can then prepare themselves to deal with it effectively or, if necessary, avoid it altogether.

Like almost all colleges and universities, the University of Chicago neither requires nor forbids faculty members to issue such warnings. Such judgments are within the core of academic freedom, and professors who feel that certain material in a course might pose a serious problem for particular students are absolutely free to alert those students in advance. Thus, despite all the fuss in the media, the University in fact has no policy prohibiting or even discouraging such warnings.

On the safe space question, the problem is one of definition, because the precise meaning of this phrase is ambiguous. What is clear, as I noted earlier, is that the University of Chicago does not itself aspire to be a safe space that shields members of our community from challenging, difficult, and sometimes unnerving issues and arguments. At the same time, though, the University fully and unequivocally supports and indeed encourages students to participate in groups and organizations that are designed to enable students with similar backgrounds, interests, and experiences to work together to discuss their shared experiences and frustrations, to test and develop their ideas, to sponsor events, and to present proposals for reform to University officials.

Indeed, the University has a broad array of such student organizations including the Asian Student Union, the Campus Crusade for Christ, the Jewish Students Association, the Latino Students Association, the Muslim Students Association, the National Organization for Women, the Native American Students Association, the Organization of Black Students, the Pro-Life Association, Queers and Associates, the South Asian Students Association, and Students for Justice in Palestine, to name just a few. These organizations are a central part of who we are, and they represent a critical part of our culture that the University enthusiastically endorses, supports, and cherishes. They are meant to be empowering, intellectually robust and, when necessary, safe.

Let me now, though, return to my central theme. Half a century ago, President Robert Maynard Hutchins asked what is it "that makes the University of Chicago a great educational institution?" The answer he gave then remains true today: "It is," he said, "the intense, strenuous and constant intellectual activity of the place. . . . Presented with many points of view, [students are] compelled to think for [themselves]. We like to think that the air is electric, and that from it the students derive an intellectual stimulation that lasts the rest of [their] lives. This," Hutchins concluded, "is education."

This is the tradition that you inherit. Your responsibility as a student at this University is to test what you are taught at every turn, to challenge your teachers, your classmates and yourselves, to choose your own values and your own beliefs. To meet this responsibility, you will have to be independent, you will have to be daring, you will have to take risks.

It is not easy to tell your professor, who has devoted years, perhaps decades, to mastering her subject, that you disagree with her latest observation or theory. But we urge you to see the discourse of this University as an incitement to risk and to boldness. If you find yourself hesitating, if your feel timid, if you wonder if it's worth it, think of the Rebels in *Abrams*. At an age not much older than you, they dared to take on the government of the United States. You certainly can take on a mere professor.

The faculty of this University ask nothing of you that they do not also ask of themselves. Even the most distinguished teacher and scholar routinely suffers frustration and failure. It is only by taking risks, by daring to ask questions no one else has ever asked, that real contributions are achieved. Thus, if your professors ask you to take risks, know that they take risks as well. As a faculty report declared twenty years ago, "at the University of Chicago, the only appropriate response to even the most withering question is not resentment, but gratitude."

Fulfilling the responsibility of academic freedom means more than challenging your classmates and your teachers; it also means challenging yourself. It means being willing to reconsider what you yourself have come to accept as true.

In 1921, after two years in prison, Mollie Steimer, one of the Abrams Rebels, was deported to the Soviet Union. It was not what she expected. Disappointed in the political and economic system she found there, Steimer again agitated against the government. Again, she was arrested, prosecuted, and convicted of sedition. In 1923, she was deported from the Soviet Union. I don't know for sure, but I rather suspect that this was an unparalleled achievement—to be convicted of sedition and deported within five years from both the United States and the Soviet Union. Whatever else one might think of her, Mollie Steimer was not afraid to reconsider her positions.

In 1919, a majority of the Supreme Court in *Abrams* rejected the bold approach of Justice Holmes and opted for a "safe" view of the First

Amendment. Fifty years later, the Supreme Court unanimously over-ruled the majority opinion in *Abrams* and, embracing Justice's Holmes's dissenting opinion, held that the government may not punish even speech that we "loathe and believe to be fraught with death" unless that speech is both intended and likely to incite imminent lawless action. To reach this result, the Court had to challenge the first principles of its predecessors and to overturn half a century of precedent.

A great University, like a successful Court, must dedicate itself to the rigorous, open-minded, unyielding search for truth. You will learn here to ask the hard questions. But it is not enough to examine the premises, beliefs and assumptions of an earlier time and find them wanting. It is too easy to dismiss those who thought that the earth was the center of the universe, that its resources were boundless, that only men should vote, that marriage is only for people of the opposite sex, or that separate could ever be equal.

You must remember that you, too, hold beliefs that your children or your children's children will rightly regard as naive, foolish, perhaps even obscene. You must be prepared to challenge your beliefs, to reform your world, just as the Rebels in Abrams struggled to reform theirs. You, too, must challenge the nature of things. . . .

As Justice Holmes mused in *Abrams*, "all life is an experiment." May your life's experiment be filled with curiosity, boldness and courage. Thank you.

Wonder and Education

Gabriel Richardson Lear

SEPTEMBER 27, 2018

Gabriel Richardson Lear is a professor of philosophy and a member of the Committee on Social Thought. She works on ancient Greek and Roman philosophy. Her book, *Happy Lives and the Highest Good: An Essay on Aristotle's "Nicomachean Ethics"* (2004), is about the relationship between morally virtuous action and theoretical contemplation in the happiest life.

. . . I said that wondering is the aim of a *liberal arts* education, the sort of education suitable for free people like you. The freedom at issue here is, to borrow Aristotle's memorable phrase, the freedom of people with "the power of choice." You have the power of choice, the authority and ability to shape your own lives and the lives of your communities. Free people need orienting ideas that help them put different aspects of their lives together into a world; but they also need the ability to face up to it when circumstances show that their ideas don't all fit together, and they need to react to this disorienting and sometimes painful experience with productive wondering, rather than with defensiveness. The dangers of confusing real wondering with either awe-filled amazement or skeptical debunking are not merely hypothetical and they are not limited to academic life. No doubt as students you have already encountered people who love to criticize the ideas of others because they thrill to the sense of victory and whose defense of "the truth" is really just an excuse to revel in a feeling of power. And you may also have encountered students who are so enamored of an idea or way of looking at the world that they will not really think about whether it is true. Perhaps you yourselves have been drawn in these directions. But what is far more troubling is that these un-wisdom-loving ways of wondering are pervasive in the intellectual culture of our country, an intellectual culture in which there often seem to be only two possibilities: refuting the ideas of others or preaching to the choir. Both of these intellectual postures are sclerotic, incapable of allowing that "aha!" moment that is so necessary for intellectual creativity and for truthfulness.

I've been thinking about what our life together at this university must be like in order to facilitate wisdom-loving wonder. Since wonder is the result of being challenged, it is important that we have a culture of speaking our minds and of tolerating, even welcoming, criticism. It is also important that we have a culture in which people are able to listen to whatever arguments and ideas they believe, in all seriousness, will help them see things in a new way. So a community that facilitates wisdom-loving wonder must also be a community of free speakers or, to put it a better way, free conversationalists.

There has been a lot of talk on this campus about free speech. Our university guarantees freedom of speech and of inquiry as a matter of right. There is no central authority that determines what teachers must, may, or may not teach; there is no central authority that vets invitations to outside speakers; and there is no central authority that determines which ideas students may or may not express. The only place the university as such will take action is with respect to people who obstruct teachers from teaching what they think should be taught and or who prevent university members from hearing and discussing ideas they have invited speakers to share.

I am in favor of the university's position on our rights to free speech and free inquiry. But we need to be very clear about something: simply having these institutional freedoms does not guarantee a good outcome. We should not make the mistake of thinking that a community in which everyone can say what they want is inevitably a community in which wonder and truth and the productive search for wisdom will flourish.

Freedom of speech is an institutional liberty, but the point of that liberty is to allow for the development and exercise of a *virtue*, a human *excellence* of speaking freely. We as a university have been thinking a lot about freedom of speech as a liberty guaranteed by governments and universities, but it seems to me we need to do a lot more thinking more about the relevant virtue. We need to think more about what free speaking is like when it is *excellent*. What I have been trying to suggest is this: The *virtue* or *excellence* of free speech is the ability to speak your mind in a *serious* conversation, and a serious conversation is the sort of conversation that leads to or springs from the experience of wondering. This ability does not develop simply on its own. Simply being protected in the *right* to speak our minds does not ensure that we will have the ability to do so *well*. We need to be thinking about what other institutional structures foster this *excellence* and we need to be thinking about how we, as individuals can get better at speaking freely in a way that leads to and from wonder.

If I were a social scientist, I might say something about institutional structures, but since I am trained in the humanities, I want to close by saying something about the images and metaphors we use to talk about free speech and its value. Lately, I've been thinking that some of the standard metaphors for a community of free speakers present a distorted image of the way an *excellent* free speaker engages in conversation. This matters, because images of our ideals shape our deliberations and behaviors in subtle ways.

Sometimes, when people defend freedom of speech, they talk about the "battlefield of ideas." This image suggests that people who speak freely are intellectual "combatants," challenging and attacking opposed ideas. But this metaphor is obviously inadequate as a way of imagining free speech as a truth-seeking activity. No one goes to war in order to find out who *should* win or where the truth about anything lies. Can you imagine a soldier who pauses on the battlefield to wonder whose side he should be fighting on? An "intellectual combatant" is someone who has already decided what to think. He aims only to change the minds of others; he is not open to the discovery that he doesn't know what he's talking about, nor will he embrace the wonderful realization that the structure of reality is something somewhat different from what either he or his "opponent" had assumed. The metaphor of intellectual combat has no place in an academic ideal of free inquiry because its "hero" is incapable of wondering.

Another common metaphor is the "free marketplace of ideas." Just as competition in the free market improves our access to good products, so too, the story goes, free debate improves our access to true ideas. Now, let us leave aside the distortion involved in viewing someone who argues for an idea as trying to sell it. There are distortions here, but since you are students you are more likely to see yourself in the role of the consumer. But there are problems here, too. A consumer typically tries to evaluate the quality of a product *before* buying it. She holds the product at arm's length, trying to make an evaluation before making a commitment. But ideas aren't like that. There's no way to understand—really understand—a complicated theory without coming to see for yourself what can be said in its favor. Taking another person's ideas seriously is not simply a matter of repeating what they say. You must understand why their way of thinking seems reasonable. Now it is possible to question and criticize ideas you learn about while standing from them at a distance. But unless you try to sympathetically enter into the other person's way of seeing, opening yourself to seeing why a reasonable person might think these ideas are true, you will not yourself be able to feel the force of whatever refutation you offer. Even if you decide the idea is a good one, if you try to evaluate before entering sympathetically into the thought, you will not wonder. Your mind may contain a collection of true ideas, but you will never have felt the friction of having your mind shaped by the world in the activity of thinking about it. Free, wisdom-seeking inquiry demands sympathetic engagement. It requires taking a bite of the apple before you've paid for it.

Once you realize that, you see that we face a dilemma. Certain ideas strike us intuitively as odious; we do not want to engage sympathetically with them, because we do not want to risk being changed by them. On the other hand, it can be hard to know in advance whether our aversion is complacent and defensive, born of an unwillingness really to think about our commitments. This is a real problem and it cannot be solved simply by saying that in a free marketplace of ideas, everything should be allowed. That metaphor tempts you to think you can be safe from thinking, because you can evaluate intellectual products before you consume them. But engaging in conversation as a consumer will close you off from the possibility of wondering. Just as we should abandon the metaphor of intellectual combat, so too I think we should set aside the metaphor of the marketplace of ideas.

Free inquiry—the sort that inspires wonder and is oriented by wonder—is a joint activity. One person may put forward her ideas and another person may criticize, but it is an attempt to think creatively *together*. This ideal of excellent free speaking requires courage, sympathy, goodwill, and trust. It is a form of intellectual friendship. You all will develop intellectual friendships here over the next four years. My hope is that you will take these friendships and the habits of serious, wondering discussion with you when you graduate to improve our civic discourse.

So I say to you again: Welcome to the University of Chicago!

The Three S's of Discovery

SELF, SOCIAL, SCIENTIFIC

Kimberly Kay Hoang

SEPTEMBER 21, 2021

Kimberly Kay Hoang is Professor of Sociology and the College and the director of Global Studies at the University of Chicago. Her research examines dealmaking in frontier and emerging economies. Dr. Hoang is the author of *Spiderweb Capitalism: How Global Elites Exploit Frontier Markets* (2022), the winner of five distinguished book awards from the Association of American Publishers and the American Sociological Association.

. . . Another key characteristic of the University of Chicago's relational experience is its emphasis on independent inquiry and freedom of expression. One of the University's fundamental values is open discourse that exposes students to multiple perspectives. The University of Chicago takes seriously the "battle of ideas" that feeds the life of the mind and drives the discovery of new knowledge.

In your journeys of social discovery, I encourage you to approach this fundamental value in a relational manner, which means seriously interrogating what freedom of expression means in "theory" versus "practice." In theory, free expression at its best is about diversity and inclusion and exposure to people from all walks of life. It is about celebrating our differences even when it makes us uncomfortable. In theory, this also assumes that we live in an equal world unfettered by power relations.

In practice as I'm sure you all realize, the reality of expression is messy, nuanced, and always relational. We know, that some voices are not only much louder, but they are also more powerful than others. The weight of that power can effectively create a silencing effect that does not foster freedom of expression on equal grounds. Indeed, it can be to lopsided or distorted as to impede the freedom of inquiry that is our raison d'être in higher education.

As a professor in the classroom environment there are many questions around the potential LIMITS of freedom of expression. Can anybody really just say whatever they want? What for example is the difference between speech that constitutes harassment, "hate speech" or "offensive speech"? If the essence is that students should expose themselves to offensive speech and create a compelling counter discourse, then in theory all students should feel capable and empowered to speak up at all times regardless of how unpopular their ideas are.

But it is also important to recognize moments when speech hinders our ability to listen to a truly diverse set of perspectives, and learn something valuable. Institutions, like the University of Chicago, are made of up people. We have our values and our cultures and now you are part of this place, and YOU will play an important role in shaping the environment around us. As you enter this space, I would invite you to think relationally about social discovery as it relates to freedom of expression. Who will be on the receiving end of your freedom of expression? Who has the power or freedom to ignore your speech and who doesn't? If we so value diversity and inclusion of all views, whose speech are you going to give weight, respect, and recognition?

Inclusion is not something that just happens, it is something that requires thoughtfulness, care, mutual recognition, and sacrificing privilege for the less privileged. It also requires that we ask ourselves: When am I talking too much? Or, am I taking up too much space? When do I need to listen more so that I too can hear and understand where my classmates are coming from? Students need to do this for "selfish" reasons too—to grow personally and intellectually.

On a relational level, this requires compassion, empathy, and understanding that the people around us are constantly evolving and are on their own journey of self-discovery. What they say—tweet or post—in one moment may not reflect who they grow to become during their time here. So, we as an intellectual community, must constantly ask what do we need to do to create a space where everyone can contribute and where all values are equally heard? We also need to be generous to each other, to foster trust on which collaborative discovery rests. . . .

Sapere Aude and *Parrhesia*— Academic Freedom and Intellectual Courage

Christopher J. Wild

SEPTEMBER 21, 2023

Christopher J. Wild is a professor in the Department of Germanic Studies and the Committee on Theater and Performance Studies, and the director of the Parrhesia Program on Public Discourse at the College. His work examines the ways in which theology and religion inform developments that are generally considered genuinely modern. His latest book is *Descartes' Meditative Turn: Cartesian Thought as Spiritual Practice* (2024).

. . . . Here at the University of Chicago we pride ourselves that we do not tell students what to think but we teach them how to think. The crux of liberal education at a place like this is not which major you choose, the disciplinary knowledge you acquire, but the intellectual virtues, the habits of mind, and the practices of deliberation, listening, and debate you develop. Most of the majors we offer are no different from other institutions. But what you can learn here is a distinctive style of thinking. And more generally, you have the opportunity to cultivate what we call here "a life of the mind." Thus, most of my colleagues would agree that it is not important which major you choose, but that you are open to have your thinking transformed.

Socrates felt education to be so transformative that he defined it as an "art of turning around" or to put it in a more familiar idiom: a conversion. After all, "conversion" is, as the Latin root reminds us, literally a "turning toward." Now you might ask: Isn't conversion a religious phenomenon? Isn't conversion like the one Paul experienced on the road to Damascus in a way the opposite of a liberal education that transforms students into independent thinkers? Doesn't conversion put someone under the spell of a religious creed and its dogmas? Well it turns out that conversion was a philosophical phenomenon and concept before it was adopted by early Christianity (and later applied to other religions). In ancient philosophy it referred first and foremost to the profound transformation of the self brought about through philosophical thought and practice. Pivotal to that transformation was the kind of turn towards oneself that Socrates made when he heeded the injunction of the Delphic oracle "Know Thyself" and began to examine his life as well as that of others. Philosophical education was conversive, because it involved letting yourself be transformed, making the knowledge and skills you learn your own, and putting what one believes to be true and right into practice. Ancient philosophy was thus less about the examination of abstract questions than a way of life based on self-reflection and -transformation, truth-seeking and -telling, and care for others. Thus, getting a liberal education is not only about acquiring and expanding your knowledge and skills, but just as importantly about coming to an understanding who you are, who you want to be, and what you want to do with your life. . . .

It is no coincidence that liberal education has its roots in ancient Athens and a few other Greek city-states that had democratic governance. To become a competent citizen within a self-ruled community needed a specific set of skills, capacities, and values that a new kind of education was designed to provide; including the ability to exercise independent and self-reflexive thought, the development of critical and informed judgment, and the skill to speak truthfully and effectively in the assembly. In short, ancient democracies depended on independently minded citizens who freely exercised their judgment and choice and unfettered by authority.

The Roman Republic inherited this association between education and liberty, and it was the famous orator Cicero who coined the term *artes liberales* or liberal arts, using the word liberal in its original Latin sense of "pertaining to free persons." His authority ensured the survival of liberal education in the middle ages, where it became organized systematically as the seven liberal arts: the *trivium*: rhetoric, grammar, and logic; and the *quadrivium*: arithmetic, geometry, astronomy, and music. While the term "liberty" does not come to mind, when thinking of the medieval cities and states that supported universities, the link between education freedom held, since its members, both faculty and students, held special rights that other townspeople and citizens lacked. Two thousand years after its emergence, Frederick Douglas still saw the same connection. When his master angrily remarked about his ability to read that "it will forever make him unfit as a slave," he recognized education as "the direct pathway from slavery to freedom"—as he later recalled.

Around the same time across the Atlantic the link between education and liberty was crucial for the emergence of the modern research university in the German lands. When Wilhelm von Humboldt, the brother of famous naturalist Alexander von Humboldt, was tasked with drafting plans for a new kind of university in Berlin, he made academic freedom the foundation of its mission of cultivating "knowledge and science in the deepest and broadest sense." What was so novel about the university Humboldt designed, was that intellectual inquiry and the production of knowledge became its all-defining rationale and purpose. Unlike lower schools (or for that matter medieval universities) which have as their purpose imparting to students "settled bodies of knowledge," this new type of university aims to produce new knowledge. Research and inquiry have as their aim the discovery of truth, and thus knowledge production should not be determined by considerations, factors, or aims external and alien to the process. Put simply, researchers and scholars go where inquiry leads them and truth is pursued for its own sake. Humboldt's "idea of pure science and scholarship" can be only realized by insisting on, what he calls, the twin principles of complete "freedom" and "autonomy."

History proved Humboldt right. His model of the modern research university was pivotal for the emergence of modern sciences and letters as it produced what a historian has called its "mandarins" such as the physicists Albert Einstein, Werner Heisenberg, and many others, chemists such as Robert Bunsen and Justus von Liebig, physicians like Robert Virchow and Robert Koch, sociologists like Max Weber, or philosophers like Hegel and even Nietzsche to name only a few. So when a group of young and ambitious scholars and scientists set out to establish a new university in the Midwest that was to be unlike the elite colleges of the East Coast that had been founded on the Anglo-Saxon model, they not surprisingly looked to the model of the Humboldt university. And today the University of Chicago is one of the model's purest incarnations in the world.

Many of you may say "What does this concept of academic freedom have to do with me?" Isn't academic freedom for privileged professors? Doesn't it pertain to things like tenure that gives them unparalleled job security? Or their right to express their opinions freely, whether in the classroom or beyond the walls of the ivory tower. In other words, academic freedom is what walls and protects the faculty from the real world. It's the ivory that makes the ivory tower.

Of course, there is some truth to this but as in any caricature it is only part of the story. Humboldt encapsulated his notion of academic freedom in the twin terms of "Lehr- und Lernfreiheit," the liberty to teach and learn. The point that I want to stress here is that academic freedom is just as much about the freedom to learn. It applies to students as much as to teachers. Only if the freedom of inquiry applies to both, can they unite in fulfilling the university's mission of unending knowledge production. In fact, Humboldt sees the relation between teacher and student as a symbiotic one, and teaching and learning as equally essential to research. Teaching should not only flow directly from the professor's research but enable it in the first place. Unfettered freedom of inquiry affords a dynamic in which teacher and student join and work together in the production of knowledge. So academic freedom belongs as much to the students as it does to teachers. It is the freedom to shape their education, to shape themselves through their education, to become the kind of thinker, knower, citizen, and human being they aspire to be. . . .

Sapere aude!, intellectual courage, is at the heart of liberal education. In fact, learning to think for yourself is what puts the "liberal" in liberal education, accounts for the "freedom" in the notion of academic freedom. It is, thus, not some abstract concept that belongs to faceless institutions, to their leaders, or to the faculty as some corporate entity; it is an intellectual virtue and civic practice that belongs to each and every member of a university's intellectual community. It comes with responsibility, namely the duty to exercise it in everything you think and do as a student in shaping yourself. And it requires intellectual and moral courage, because thinking and learning independently comes with considerable risk. . . .

As Socrates found out for himself, truth-telling can be risky, even deadly business.

Athenians had a name for such truth-telling. In ancient Athens every citizen had the right to speak before the assembly. That right was called *isegoria*. But Athenians also recognized that speaking before the assembly was not without risk and required courage. Thus, they also had a term for availing oneself of the right to speak and stepping up to tell the truth to an audience who might not want to hear it. And that term was *parrhesia* and the person who speaks freely and fearlessly in order to tell the truth they believe in, the truth-teller was called *parrhesiastes*. *Isegoria* is the right but *parrhesia* is the practice to speak freely. And the way the term was understood made clear that the Greeks recognized that speaking freely and truthfully could be difficult and potentially perilous, because the truth could upset or anger the listener.

The courage to speak the truth freely, to deliberate and dialogue fearlessly with and before others, is an essential dimension of the intellectual courage at the heart of academic freedom. *Parrhesia* is the twin of Kant's *sapere aude* and Socrates's "know thyself." Without vigorous deliberation and dialogue an intellectual community devoted to the pursuit of truth and the production of knowledge cannot function and flourish. Thus, all its members are called upon to listen and understand, interrogate and test, deliberate and debate ideas, thoughts, theories, views that are generated through research, inquiry, and learning. All that makes intuitive sense. But the distinction *between* isegoria and *parrhesia* recognizes that there is a difference, even a gulf between an abstract right and a concrete practice; that the former is an indispensable precondition that remains incomplete without its enactment; an enactment that requires courage, skill, and frequent practice—which the Athenians captured with the term *parrhesia*.

Given Chicago's Humboldtian legacy, free inquiry and open discourse have been a keystone of the University's academic culture from the very beginning. Its first president William Rainey Harper installed the "the principle of complete freedom of speech on all subjects" as one of the foundations of the University; and his successors have regularly renewed this principle until today.

Less than a decade ago the University's late president Robert Zimmer appointed a faculty committee to reaffirm our "commitment to free, robust, and uninhibited debate and deliberation among all members of the University's community." The committee's report quickly became known as the "Chicago Principles," and I hope you had a chance to read it in advance of today's address.

The Chicago Principles are our version of the Athenian *isegoria*. They guarantee academic freedom across the University, giving everyone license to speak freely in the pursuit of truth and knowledge. They are invaluable and indispensable for everything we do, for research and scholarship as well as teaching and mentoring, and the many other functions of the university. But they remain abstract and lifeless and with little impact on the university's intellectual life if they are not put into practice. In fact, dozens of universities and colleges have adopted the Chicago Principles often almost word for word, and in many cases arguably without palpable effect on their academic culture. Thus, they too require *parrhesia* to come alive, to be practiced by every member of our intellectual community, whether it is in the classroom, on the quad, in the residence halls, or in the myriad other spaces and venues, real and virtual, that make up the university.

What better way is there to practice *parrhesia* and to heed Kant's *sapere aude* than by pausing for a moment and refraining from blindly following the Chicago Principles? What better way to put the Chicago Principles into practice than by examining and debating them? So let me close by getting such a critical examination started; an examination that I invite you to continue with your peers in the break-out discussion following this address.

As a literature professor I always begin with looking at the title of a text, which in this case is not Chicago Principles but "Report of the Committee on Freedom of Expression." The focus on free expression is echoed by the already quoted proclamation by William Rainey Harper in the first paragraph and then appears throughout. But let me ask whether freedom of speech in an academic context is really complete and absolute? Is freedom of expression really the highest principle within a university like ours?

I am not thinking here of the limitations to free expression that the report contemplates, such as the restriction of illegal speech, defamation, genuine threats and harassment, the substantial violation of privacy and confidentiality, and speech that is "incompatible with the functioning of the University."

Rather, I can imagine many quotidian spaces and situations in which you and I cannot simply utter just anything without constraints and consequences. Take the classroom, for example. If you are a student in one of my sections of "Greece and Rome" and you say something that has nothing to do with our class discussion or doesn't pertain to the subject of the course, I'll politely point that out, but if you do it again and again, it will have consequences, for instance on your participation grade. But even if what you say is germane to the topic we are discussing but lacks textual support, and you insist on it despite the contrary evidence provided by your class mates or me, it will affect your participation grade. That applies to me as the instructor, too. If I spend all of my class time telling my students about my latest vacations or talking about party politics, my students will note that in my evaluations and may even complain to the College; and at some point my department chair or my dean will remind me of my duties.

The same goes for a faculty member who gives an academic lecture or talk. The mission of a research university is to advance knowledge

beyond the boundaries of established consensus through open intellectual exchange. This involves the testing of old ideas as well as the open-
ended exploration of entirely new ones based on verifiable evidence.
Similarly, students are not only taught the settled knowledge of a given
discipline but ideally how the process of extending that knowledge
works. Now the point of this process is to advance knowledge, not just
discuss whatever comes to mind. It is true that scholars and scientists
regularly question the assumptions of a discipline, at times returning
to seemingly obsolete views. But consistently doubting and challenging settled knowledge will at some point exclude one from the community of scholars and scientists. To put it simply, once the validity of facts
and views has been established through a long and laborious process of
testing, they are no longer subject to unfettered debate in an academic
context—unless new evidence presents itself. Statements that obstruct
or don't further the pursuit of truth and production of knowledge are
not strictly illegal but are sanctioned by the academic community in a
variety of ways. Robert Hutchins, one of the University's great presidents, is thus correct that in theory "our students [as well as our faculty]
should have the freedom to discuss any problem that presents itself,"
but in practice classroom communication and scientific discourse follow rules and procedures somewhat different from those of public debate. That's why the term academic freedom seems more apt; and we
put the "inquiry" before "expression" in the University's new "Forum
for Free Inquiry and Expression" that will be officially launched in a
little over two weeks.

Having said that, there are many spaces and situations in the
University that are not directly tied to inquiry and the production of
knowledge: the dorms and dining halls for example. And what about
the quad, hallways, and the many other spaces in between? Are they governed by academic freedom or by principles and values governing the
public sphere beyond the university? In other words, can one say more
and at the same time less? And what about the many smaller communities and social groupings within the university? Who decides how they
should interact and communicate with each other? These are all open
questions that call for deliberation and debate.

When the report states that "as a corollary to the University's commitment to protect and promote free expression, members of the University community must also act in conformity with the principle of free expression," it seems to suggest that the Chicago Principles are not themselves open to deliberation and debate. But I hope that I have persuaded you that they are subject to the same paradox as Kant's *sapere aude*, namely that we truly enact them by critically interrogating and questioning them. . . .

committee reports

On the University's Role in Political and Social Action

THE KALVEN COMMITTEE

*A report by a faculty committee
chaired by Harry Kalven Jr.*

NOVEMBER 3, 1967

The Kalven report, named after the distinguished First Amendment scholar who served as its chair, came at a tumultuous time for the nation's universities. The University of Chicago was no exception. As the Vietnam War raged, and movements for racial and social justice gained momentum, students made a number of demands of the University. Particularly acute were demands that the University stop providing class rankings to the Selective Service, and to divest from South Africa as well as from companies in the military-industrial complex. The committee met between February and May and achieved a consensus on much of the report. However, there was internal disagreement about the scope of inevitable exceptions. The report treats two contexts constituting "extraordinary instances," in which the University could or must speak. One is when the University acts in its corporate capacity and of necessity must take positions. The other context arises in crises that threaten the very mission and free expression values of the university. In the event of such crises, the report states a requirement for action: "It becomes the obligation of the university as an institution . . . to defend its interests and its values." Gilbert White preferred a broader scope for speaking out in exceptional cases, seeking to include "instances where the public significance is large or where the University's influence is clearly strong."[1] George Stigler disagreed, and Harry Kalven drafted a compromise.[2] Stigler included an addendum to lay out his position. The precise scope of exceptions and obligations continues to be debated in an era in which university statements have become the norm at many institutions.

The Committee was appointed in February 1967 by President George W. Beadle and requested to prepare "a statement on the University's role in political and social action." The Committee conceives its function as principally that of providing a point of departure for discussion in the University community of this important question.

The Committee has reviewed the experience of the University in such matters as its participation in neighborhood redevelopment, its defense of academic freedom in the Broyles Bill inquiry of the 1940s and again in the Jenner Committee hearings of the early 1950s, its opposition to the Disclaimer Affidavit in the National Defense Education Act of 1958, its reappraisal of the criteria by which it rents the off-campus housing it owns, and its position on furnishing the rank of male students to Selective Service. In its own discussions, the Committee has found a deep consensus on the appropriate role of the university in political and social action. It senses some popular misconceptions about that role and wishes, therefore, simply to reaffirm a few old truths and a cherished tradition.

A university has a great and unique role to play in fostering the development of social and political values in a society. The role is defined by the distinctive mission of the university and defined too by the distinctive characteristics of the university as a community. It is a role for the long term.

The mission of the university is the discovery, improvement, and dissemination of knowledge. Its domain of inquiry and scrutiny includes all aspects and all values of society. A university faithful to its mission will provide enduring challenges to social values, policies, practices, and institutions. By design and by effect, it is the institution which creates discontent with the existing social arrangements and proposes new ones. In brief, a good university, like Socrates, will be upsetting.

The instrument of dissent and criticism is the individual faculty member or the individual student. The university is the home and sponsor of critics; it is not itself the critic. It is, to go back once again to the classic phrase, a community of scholars. To perform its mission in the society, a university must sustain an extraordinary environment of freedom of inquiry and maintain an independence from political fashions, passions, and pressures. A university, if it is to be true to its faith in intellectual inquiry, must embrace, be hospitable to, and encourage the widest diversity of views within its own community. It is a community but only for the limited, albeit great, purposes of teaching and research. It is not a club, it is not a trade association, it is not a lobby.

Since the university is a community only for these limited and distinctive purposes, it is a community which cannot take collective action on the issues of the day without endangering the conditions for its existence and effectiveness. There is no mechanism by which it can reach a collective position without inhibiting that full freedom of dissent on which it thrives. It cannot insist that all of its members favor a given view of social policy; if it takes collective action, therefore, it does so at the price of censuring any minority who do not agree with the view adopted. In brief, it is a community which cannot resort to majority vote to reach positions on public issues.

The neutrality of the university as an institution arises then not from a lack of courage nor out of indifference and insensitivity. It arises out of respect for free inquiry and the obligation to cherish a diversity of viewpoints. And this neutrality as an institution has its complement in the fullest freedom for its faculty and students as individuals to participate in political action and social protest. It finds its complement, too, in the obligation of the university to provide a forum for the most searching and candid discussion of public issues.

Moreover, the sources of power of a great university should not be misconceived. Its prestige and influence are based on integrity and intellectual competence; they are not based on the circumstance that it may be wealthy, may have political contacts, and may have influential friends.

From time to time instances will arise in which the society, or segments of it, threaten the very mission of the university and its values of free inquiry. In such a crisis, it becomes the obligation of the university as an institution to oppose such measures and actively to defend its interests and its values. There is another context in which questions as to the appropriate role of the university may possibly arise, situations involving university ownership of property, its receipt of funds, its awarding of honors, its membership in other organizations. Here, of necessity, the university, however it acts, must act as an institution in its corporate capacity. In the exceptional instance, these corporate activities of the university may appear so incompatible with paramount social values as to require careful assessment of the consequences.

These extraordinary instances apart, there emerges, as we see it, a heavy presumption against the university taking collective action or expressing opinions on the political and social issues of the day, or modifying its corporate activities to foster social or political values, however compelling and appealing they may be.

These are admittedly matters of large principle, and the application of principle to an individual case will not be easy.

It must always be appropriate, therefore, for faculty or students or administration to question, through existing channels such as the Committee of the Council or the Council, whether in light of these principles the University in particular circumstances is playing its proper role.

Our basic conviction is that a great university can perform greatly for the betterment of society. It should not, therefore, permit itself to be diverted from its mission into playing the role of a second-rate political force or influence.

Harry Kalven, Jr., *Chairman*
John Hope Franklin
Gwin J. Kolb
George Stigler

Jacob Getzels
Julian Goldsmith
Gilbert F. White

Special Comment by Mr. Stigler

I agree with the report as drafted, except for the statements in the fifth paragraph from the end as to the role of the university when it is acting in its corporate capacity. As to this matter, I would prefer the statement in the following form:

> The university when it acts in its corporate capacity as employer and property owner should, of course, conduct its affairs with honor. The university should not use these corporate activities to foster any moral or political values because such use of its facilities will impair its integrity as the home of intellectual freedom.

On the Criteria of Academic Appointment

A report by a University of Chicago faculty committee

In July 1970, President Levi convened a committee under the leadership of distinguished sociologist Edward Shils to articulate and consolidate various practices related to hiring and promotion. After producing an initial report, it was reconvened in 1971 to elaborate on the question of political criteria. This was obviously a time of great ferment in American society, and many students, young faculty, and faculty candidates had been intensively engaged in political activity. The report makes clear that the central criterion for appointment and promotion in the faculty is scholarly excellence. Neither race nor gender nor political orientation, nor any other factor, are to be considered, apart from the question of whether the person will do high-quality work in scholarship and teaching in the future. Importantly, the report recognizes the potential risks of giving undue weight to seniority and of adhering to a particular scholarly tradition. It is an elegant statement of the central and dispositive importance of inquiry.

I. Introduction

The existence of the University of Chicago is justified if it achieves and maintains superior quality in its performance of the three major functions of universities in the modern world.[1] These functions are: (1) the discovery of important new knowledge; (2) the communication of that knowledge to students and the cultivation in them of the understanding and skills which enable them to engage in the further pursuit of knowledge; and (3) the training of students for entry into professions which require for their practice a systematic body of specialized knowledge.

In intellectual matters, at least, the whole amounts to more than the sum of the parts in isolation. A university faculty is not merely an assemblage of individual scientists and scholars; it must possess a corporate life and an atmosphere created by the research, teaching, and conversation of individual scientists and scholars which stimulates and sustains the work of colleagues and students at the highest possible level. Research, teaching, and training are the work of individuals. These individuals depend for their effectiveness, at least in part, on the University's provision of material and administrative services which enable their work to go on; they depend also on the maintenance in the University of an atmosphere of stimulation, tolerance, and critical openness to new ideas. The function of appointive bodies is to bring to the academic staff of the University individuals who will perform at the highest level the functions of research, teaching, and training and the maintenance of the intellectual community of the University. A university which does not perform at this level will lose its standing in the world and therewith its power to attract outstanding faculty members and outstanding students. Its failure to attract them will in turn reduce the quality of its performance. Every appointment of a mediocre candidate makes it more difficult to bring outstanding students to the university. This is why scrupulous insistence on the most demanding criteria in the act of appointment is so decisive for the University.

The conception of the proper tasks of the University determines the criteria which should govern the appointment, retention, and promotion of members of the academic staff. The criteria which are to be applied in the case of appointments to the University of Chicago should, therefore, be criteria which give preference above all to actual and prospective scholarly and scientific accomplishment of the highest order, actual and prospective teaching accomplishment of the highest order, and actual and prospective contribution to the intellectual quality of the University through critical stimulation of others within the University to produce work of the highest quality.

The University of Chicago should not aim to be a pantheon of dead or dying gods. Appointments to the University should not be made solely on the basis of past achievements but only to the degree that past achievements promise future achievement.

The tradition of the University of Chicago has defined it, primarily but not exclusively, as a research university of the highest international standing. The University of Chicago is, by its tradition, an institution where research is done by academic staff and where students are trained to do research, by induction into the state of mind and disposition to do research on important subjects and with original results. Undergraduate teaching at the University of Chicago has been and must be conducted in a way which arouses in students their capacity for discrimination and disciplined curiosity so that upon reaching the latter years of their training they will have the skills, knowledge, discrimination, and motivation to make original discoveries or will begin to be ready for the effective performance of roles in society where these qualities will bear fruit.

In the performance of its functions in research and in professional training, it becomes necessary to appoint supporting staff who are indispensable to the performance of these functions but who are not qualified for appointment to the University faculty. This raises serious problems for the University in its effort to keep to its major tasks at the level its traditions and aspirations demand.

II. Procedural Matters

A. CRITERIA

Any appointive body must have a standard by which it assesses the merits of the alternative candidates before it. Academic appointive bodies in general, and at the University of Chicago in particular, must have clearly perceived standards which they seek to apply to particular cases. They must seek to choose candidates who can conform most closely with these standards in their most exigent application. The standards to be applied by any appointive body should be those which assess the quality of performance in (1) research; (2) teaching and training, including the supervision of graduate students; (3) contribution to intellectual community; and (4) services.[2] Distinguished performance in any one of these categories does not automatically entail distinguished performance in the others. For this reason, weighting of the various criteria cannot be avoided by appointive bodies. The Committee thinks that the criterion of distinction in research should be given the greatest weight.

B. THE APPLICATION OF CRITERIA

All academic appointments to University faculties must be treated with great seriousness.[3] They should, wherever it is at all possible, be made on the basis of careful study by members of the appointive body of the publications and other written work of the candidate, and of written assessments, where desirable, by outside referees or consultants which assess originality, rigor, and fundamental significance of the work and which estimate the likelihood that the candidate is or will become a leading figure in his field. They also should be made on the most careful consideration of his teaching ability, which includes the ability to contribute effectively to the research of graduate students.

Appointive bodies should take into account the observations and written opinions of those who have observed or experienced the candidate's teaching or who have observed its results in the accomplishments of his students. They should be made on the basis of the best available information about the candidate's contribution to the intellectual activity of the university where he has worked previously in addition to his publications and his success with his students in their doctoral and subsequent research, as attested by their dissertations and publications.

All appointments, whether they are first appointments to instructorships or assistant professorships, or reappointments to assistant professorships, or promotions to permanent tenure at the level of associate professorship, or promotions from the rank of associate professor to that of professor, or appointments from outside the University to associate professorship, or extension beyond the age of normal retirement, must be conducted with the same thorough deliberation, the same careful study of relevant documentation and other evidence, and the same process of consultation. No decisions to appoint, retain, or promote between any grades should under any circumstances be regarded as "automatic."

Junior appointments of candidates who have just finished graduate work to instructorships or assistant professorships do, however, have a character of their own. The candidate's written work is likely to be scanty and may not even be available. There may be little or no evidence of his teaching, and it may be difficult to disentangle his originality from that of his professors. In such cases, all available evidence must be examined just as in other cases, but there cannot be the same certitude of judgment. For this reason, appointive bodies must always be quite explicit in stating that such an initial appointment is for a limited term.

There must be no consideration of sex, ethnic or national characteristics, or political or religious beliefs or affiliations in any decision regarding appointment, promotion, or reappointment at any level of the academic staff.

Particular care must be taken to keep "inbreeding" at a minimum. "Inbreeding" at the level of appointment to the rank of instructor and assistant professor is a temptation because the internal candidate is already known to the appointive body. The arguments against "inbreeding" are: (1) the dangers of relaxation of standards; (2) the dangers of narrowing and stereotyping the intellectual focus of the department in question; and (3) the dangers of appointing candidates who are excessively dependent intellectually on their former teachers' ideas and even presence. These are arguments to be taken seriously by appointive bodies. Nonetheless, the barrier against "inbreeding" should not be insuperable. Whenever an "inbred" candidate is considered, great pains must be taken to identify and examine with the utmost care the credentials of external candidates of high quality so that internal candidates can be properly compared with external candidates. Special emphasis should be given to external assessments in decisions which entail "inbreeding." Where, after severe scrutiny, the internal candidate is very clearly superior in his estimated potentiality as an original scientist or scholar to any of the external candidates, and if he is not only superior to his immediate competitors but is deemed likely to become an outstanding figure in his subject, the objections to "inbreeding" should be overcome in that instance.

Decisions regarding retention or promotion must deliberately eschew considerations of convenience, friendship, or congeniality. No decision to retain or promote should permit the entry of considerations of the avoidance of hardship which might confront the candidate if a favorable decision is not made. Similarly, favorable decisions to retain or promote should not be rendered on the grounds that evidence is not sufficient for a negative or positive estimate of future accomplishment. The insufficiency of such evidence is in such cases indicative of the candidate's insufficient productivity.

No appointments should ever be made in which the chief or major argument is that "outside" funds would accompany the appointment sufficient to relieve the regular budget of the cost of the appointment. Similarly, no appointment should ever be made on the initiative of a person or body from outside the University who offers to defray all expenses, salary, etc. on condition of a particular person's appointment.

Care must be taken to avoid undue regard for the rights of seniority in promotion. Consideration should be given only to quality of performance, and age should be disregarded. Thus the fact that an older member of a department or one with a longer period of service remains an associate professor should not be permitted to inhibit the promotion of a younger person to full professorship; similarly, in promotions of assistant professors the age of the candidate in relation to the age of his colleagues at the same rank should not be considered in any decision.

Great caution must be exercised by appointive committees themselves to prevent their being "stampeded" by the prestige or influence of contemporaneity. There has for some years been an increasing tendency for universities to concern themselves in their teaching and research with contemporary events—especially in the social sciences and humanities—and it is perfectly understandable that this should occur. With this focus of attention, however, there has also been a corresponding tendency to regard participants in the contemporary events as qualified to become academic staff members on the ground that their presence in the university will bring to the university the immediate experience of those events. Appointive bodies must remember that universities are, insofar as their major intellectual functions are concerned, places for scientific and scholarly analysis and training in such analysis, not theatres for the acquisition of vicarious experiences. Proposals to appointive bodies urging them to consider present or recent public notables for academic appointments must be responded to by strict adherence to the criteria of academic appointment. Where rare exceptions to this rule are permissible, such appointments must not be classified as appointments to the faculty.

These observations should not be interpreted to mean that a candidate who hitherto has not been wholly or at all in the academic profession should be automatically excluded from consideration. It means only that appointive bodies must be certain to apply the same high standards of distinction of scholarly and scientific performance to these candidates as they would to any others.

C. MODE OF ARRIVING AT DECISIONS

At present there is a wide variation among the various schools and departments of the University in the composition of their appointive bodies and in the sequence of stages of the appointive process. There is no need for uniformity, other than that recommendations for appointment (retention, promotion, extension) should originate within departments and schools, pass to the dean of the division or school, and thence to the Provost and President for approval or rejection or reference back for further consideration.

The Committee recommends that departments, schools, and committees in the University make arrangements whereby all faculty members, irrespective of rank within the department,[4] possess a voice in the appointment of new members. When it is a matter involving reappointment or promotion of existing faculty members, e.g., the reappointment or promotion of assistant professors, it is reasonable for those at the same level or below not to have a voice in the decision. The same documentation on prospective appointments which is available to senior members and external assessors should normally be available to junior members of the academic staff.

The Committee recommends that the various departments and schools of the University should establish rules which they regard as appropriate in inviting and considering the assessments of candidates for appointment made in a consultative capacity by students. The Committee is of the view that advisory student assessment of candidates for appointment should be taken seriously, particularly with regard to teaching performance and graduate supervision. The *Statutes* of the University and the obligations of the departments and schools in the performance of the three main functions of universities preclude the membership of students with voting powers on appointive bodies.

External assessors should be selected very meticulously. They should not be chosen perfunctorily or in anticipation of an assessment favoring a particular candidate. The Committee does not recommend that external assessors be invited to become formal members of appointive bodies or that they be invited to be present at interviews of candidates. It does recommend that the external assessors be provided with full documentation such as bibliographies, offprints, etc., just as provision should be made for all members of appointive bodies. At the same time, it points out that external assessors are sometimes more indulgent in their view of candidates for appointments at other universities than they are at their own. One procedure which might be followed is to request the external assessor to indicate whether he would support the appointment of the candidate at his own university to the same rank for which he is being considered at the University of Chicago. Supplementary oral consultation with assessors by telephone would be useful.

The Committee suggests that some designated members of appointive bodies, whenever an appointment is to be recommended, present their assessments of competing candidates in independently written statements as well as orally. These written assessments, together with the vote taken in the appointive body, should be sent to the dean of the division together with the recommendation.

Appointive committees should not consider only one candidate at any one time for a given appointment. It should be a firm rule, followed as frequently as possible when there is an appointment to be made, that several alternative candidates be considered. Although difficulties might be encountered because not all the candidates considered might be willing to accept appointment, this practice would lend rigor to appointive procedures. This same procedure should always be followed when an assistant professor is being considered for reappointment for a second term or for promotion to an associate professorship. At this point, he should be considered as if it were a new appointment. It should be made clear that no appointments carry with them the assurance of reappointment or promotion.

The decision to appoint an assistant professor for a second term (of two or three years) should be made only if there is reasonable confidence that at the end of that period he is likely to be qualified for promotion to the rank of associate professorship. In considering internal candidates for retention or promotion (or extension), members of appointive bodies must be willing to recognize that their earlier assessments might have been wrong. The effectiveness of the University in the performance of its intellectual functions would be diminished by the repetition of earlier erroneous assessments.

D. SPECIAL SITUATIONS

The foregoing remarks accept the principle that the power of formal recommendation of appointment rests with the faculty members of departments and committees and schools. This is the general practice, established by tradition and convention, and it should be adhered to. There are, however, occasionally special situations where deviation from this practice is necessary.

Where the quality of work of a department, school, or committee has declined over the years, special weight should be given to the views of external assessors regarding any candidate whose appointment has been internal proposed. Where a field, subject or department is expiring because first-class intellects are not available to constitute its staff, the discontinuation or suspension of the department should be considered.

One way to deal with the situation of a deteriorated department or, what is quite a different situation, of a department which has too few professors to make the necessary judgment about optimal lines of development, is for the dean of the division to appoint an ad hoc committee of distinguished persons from other universities and from adjacent departments in the University of Chicago to canvass the field and make recommendations for appointments and promotions. Another way is for the president or provost to appoint a new chairman with powers greater than those ordinarily enjoyed by chairmen.

E. TERMS OF APPOINTMENT

Initial appointments to the rank of instructor or assistant professor should be treated variously. In some cases the evidence at hand may be strong enough to indicate that the candidate may well be a strong prospect for permanent tenure. In this case an initial appointment as assistant professor for a term of four years is advantageous. (This is within the present provision of the University *Statutes*.[5]) This would have the advantage that the next decision would be taken after a period of three years rather than the present period of two years for a three-year term of appointment. The latter term is often too short for the accumulation of sufficient evidence on the intellectual promise of the candidate.

In other cases, an initial appointment is based largely on recommendations of the candidates from outside graduate schools so that an initial appointment for two or three years, given the possibility of reappointment, may be most appropriate. In some departments it should be possible as a matter of general practice to offer junior appointments with the explicit understanding that the appointment is strictly a terminal appointment and that most or all of those so appointed will leave the University at the end of that term. Such arrangements have certain advantages in promoting a flow of young talent, in taking care of certain teaching and service obligations, in training young postdoctoral students here, and in assisting the flow of scholarly information. Moreover, the University remains free to appoint the very best of such persons in more permanent ways.

In many ways, the promotion to rank of associate professor and to permanent tenure is the one requiring greatest care and consideration.

Promotion to the rank of professorship from associate professorship should not be automatic either on the basis of seniority or after the lapse of a specified period of time. Promotion to professorship within the University should be made on the basis of the same procedures as appointments to full professorship from outside the University. . . .

. . . In this connection, it is sometimes important to take into account the effect of retirement upon the general strength of the department. If, for example, several retirements are scheduled to take place concurrently and prospects for adequate replacement are not favorable, the department involved might be threatened by serious depletion of its staff within a single year. In such cases, it may be desirable to "stagger" the retirement of senior faculty members by appropriate extension of their appointment.

In view of the fact that academic members of the University sometimes make arrangements several years before the age of normal retirement to resign in order to go to another university where the age of retirement is later, it might be desirable for the University that such decisions regarding extension may be made as many as two years prior to the age of normal retirement. (The arrangement for the supervision of dissertations also counsels a decision prior to the last year of normal tenure.)

The Committee discussed the possibility of an age of "early retirement" with modified pension provisions. It also discussed instances in which, for various reasons, a faculty member's association with the University should be terminated before the statutory age of retirement. The Committee noted precedents for such a procedure in other universities and recommends that where a faculty member on permanent tenure shows no promise of continuing usefulness to the University, the termination of his appointment be given serious consideration. Such "early retirement" may be made possible through either modified pension provisions or the "commutation" of full-term appointment by a lump-sum payment of anticipated future salary.

The Committee recommends that there should be a category of strictly temporary appointment for which there is not only the usual terminal contract of appointment but explicit statement to the appointee that the appointment will not extend past a particular date. These short-term appointments should be used only on special occasions, such as emergencies where there is no regular member of the academic staff available to teach a particular subject which must be taught. If a person is on an emergency short-term appointment and is considered for regular appointment at the end of the period of his emergency appointment, his candidacy should be treated like any outside candidacy. (These observations do not apply to the short-term appointments of visiting professors and lecturers. To these appointments the same criteria apply as to normal appointments.)

F. CONDITIONS OF APPOINTMENT

All academic appointments, when confirmed by the provost, president, and Board of Trustees, should be notified by letter to the appointee, stipulating that his acceptance of the appointment places him under obligation to "conduct and supervise research, teach, and contribute to the intellectual life of the University."

G. UNIFORMITY OF APPLICATION OF CRITERIA

A question has repeatedly been raised concerning the differing standards which seem to be applied to faculty members whose primary duties are in the College and those whose primary duties are in the divisions. Those in the latter category are judged primarily by their research accomplishments. The application of these same criteria for promotion and permanent tenure to those who are burdened with teaching does not seem to be fair. The existence of dual standards cannot be avoided as long as these two categories exist. The only way to abolish the dual standard is to abolish one of the categories by abolishing the differences in the kinds of tasks performed by members of the faculty.

The three criteria for appointment to the University of Chicago—distinction in research, distinction in teaching, distinction in intellectual contribution to the University as an intellectual community—should be applied in all situations in which appointments must be made. In general, as has already been stated, the criterion of distinction in research should be weighted most heavily. The University of Chicago faces a peculiar dilemma, however. It arises from the fact that at least since the 1930s, and more acutely over the past quarter of a century, there have been integrated into the structure of the University, two not wholly harmonious modes of weighting the criteria of research and teaching. Appointees to the University faculty posts in divisional departments, schools, and committees have been selected primarily according to the criterion of distinction in research; the other criterion was applied but given secondary significance. Appointees to the College have in certain fields been selected primarily according to the criterion of prospective teaching performance and promoted in accordance with evidence of distinction in teaching. The research criterion has not been disregarded, but it has not been given primacy or even equal weight.

These divergent weightings of the criteria have resulted in a degree of stratification in the University which is injurious, and various efforts have been made to overcome this stratification by various departments. Some of these efforts have apparently been successful; in others they have introduced an unassimilated mass of persons who do not share the intellectual aims of their colleagues and who believe they have no future in the University. In still others, stratification has been contained with good grace on both sides, but even in such fortunate outcomes, the fact remains the same: the criteria have been applied with different weightings and they have, therefore, constituted two different sets of criteria.

The Committee believes that normally appointment should involve both teaching and research and that candidates should be judged on both qualities. Appointive bodies should discourage appointments for research alone or for teaching alone. In particular, College appointments should not carry teaching loads so heavy as to preclude productive research activity.

H. JOINT APPOINTMENTS

It is one of the merits of the University of Chicago that it has often led in the development of new subjects through the freedom of its members to conduct interdisciplinary research and teaching. "Joint appointments" have been one of the devices by which this kind of work has been fostered, and the Committee views such arrangements with favor. These joint appointments have, however, sometimes led to grave difficulties for both the individual holding the appointment and for the University. Primarily because of administrative problems and faculty politics, there have been cases where persons have held appointments with full privileges in one department but were denied the privileges associated with the appointment in another department. Joint appointments should enjoy the full privileges of the respective organizations, according to the level of appointment. Appointments initiated by institutes, interdisciplinary committees, etc. should be made as joint appointments with one of the teaching departments, and no members of the faculty should be able to find shelter from teaching by virtue of institute or committee appointments alone.

Joint appointments often present difficulties for junior members at the time of their reappointment or promotion. They find themselves in "double jeopardy." Each department applies the criteria for advancement in its own way, and each exacts its own full set of demands independently of the other. Hence it is important to protect the joint appointee by not demanding twice the commitment of service on committees, examinations, etc. expected of normal appointments in a single department.

The Committee wishes to emphasize that when such appointments are made, each department participating should treat the appointment, whether it is from within or outside the University, with the same stringency as it would treat an appointment entirely within its own jurisdiction. The Committee is especially concerned that the fact that a department's share of a joint appointee's services in research and teaching is not paid for from its own budget should not cause the appointive process to be treated perfunctorily. Agreements to share in a joint appointment of a candidate wholly paid for from another unit's budget should not encourage its treatment as a matter of "courtesy." Research associates are not members of the University faculty entitled to the prerogatives of faculty members, except where, as holders of joint appointments, they enjoy the title of "research associate (with rank of . . .)" in one of the departments.[6] Research associateships do, however, fall into the category of academic appointments. For this reason, the Committee believes that their appointments should be reviewed periodically by the appointive bodies of departments, to ensure that the criterion of distinction in research is strictly adhered to. This would also render less likely the possibility that a research associate will become so "embedded" in the department that he is retained until the age of retirement or until he is recommended for faculty appointment.

III. Criteria

A. RESEARCH

The criteria of appointment are implicit in the definition of the aims of the University of Chicago. The traditions of the University of Chicago in which these aims are contained place it under the obligation to be in the first rank of the universities of the world in all those subjects and fields in which it is active. This means that appointive bodies must seek to recruit to its staff and to retain on its staff persons whose accomplishments and potentialities are adjudged to be of the very highest order in research and in teaching and in the creation of an intellectual environment in which research of the highest order is done and in which students of distinguished intellectual potentiality are formed and guided.

The Committee regards distinction in research accomplishment and promise as the *sine qua non* of academic appointment. Even where a candidate offers promise of being a classroom teacher of outstanding merit, evidence should be sought as to the promise of distinction in his research capacity. Even if his research production is small in amount, no compromise should be made regarding the quality of the research done.

The appointment of academic staff members must, therefore, place in the forefront the criteria which will populate the University with persons capable of research at the most advanced level and of the highest quality.

It is imperative that in every case the appointive body ask itself whether the candidate proposed, if young, is likely in a decade to be among the most distinguished scientists or scholars of his generation; if middle-aged whether he is already in that position and whether the work which he is likely to do in the remainder of his career will be of at least the same quality.

In the recruitment of new staff members, emphasis should be placed upon the recruitment of younger persons who have not yet reached the height of their potentialities.

Young staff members should be encouraged to do research in spite of the importance and pressure of their teaching. At the same time, appointive bodies must be on the alert against the dangers of appointing young persons in a way which forces them into research projects in which they have no genuine interest.

To offset the handicaps which might arise from concentration on undergraduate teaching, University departments should make a more determined effort to rotate their undergraduate teaching responsibilities so that junior members of the faculty can be provided with more time for research, especially when it is requested.

When older, very distinguished persons outside the University are considered for appointment, the major emphasis should be on their prospective intellectual influence in the University through teaching and informal contact with colleagues and students, as well as on the likelihood of a continued high quality of their own research. These same observations apply in general to candidacy of any person will past his middle age.

While stressing the preponderant importance of the appointment of young persons, the Committee recognizes that exceptions must sometimes be allowed. Thus, sometimes if there has been a disproportionate number of retirements or resignations by eminent senior members of a department, candidates at the same level of seniority and eminence might be sought by the appointive body. The need to maintain the prestige of the department and to render it attractive to outstanding younger persons would justify making this exception to the recommended emphasis on the appointment of younger persons.

It is obvious that sheer quantity of scholarly or scientific production, if of indifferent quality, must never be permitted to be counted in favor of any appointment. In assessing the research accomplishments of a particular candidate, adequate regard should be given to the extent to which his original intellectual or research accomplishments are contained in the work of research students and junior colleagues. Nonetheless, it is the quality of the actual publications, or the likelihood of such, which must be given the primary weight in assessment of research accomplishment and potentiality.

Appointive committees, in seeking out candidates and in making their decisions, should bear in mind the prospective development of the subjects on which the candidates have been working. They must seek to appoint a sufficient number of members of the department whose interests and skills are complementary to each other's, so that students will obtain a well-rounded training in their respective fields and so that there will be sufficient mutual stimulation within the department. At the same time, the appointive committees must be alert to the dangers of narrowing the range of intellectual interests represented in their respective departments.

Appointive committees in considering candidates should reflect not only on the candidate's capacity for development to eminence in his subject but the prospective vitality and continued significance of the candidate's main interest. It is important that departments should not become graveyards for subjects which have lost their importance. Thus, appointive committees in seeking out and considering candidates should, while regarding present or prospective distinction as indispensable, attend to the needs of the department in the various subfields within the discipline or subject and the capacity of those subfields for further scientific or scholarly development. Just as research projects should not be undertaken simply because money is available for them in substantial amounts, so there should be no academic appointments simply to staff a particular project.

B. TEACHING

Teaching at various levels and in various forms is one of the central functions of the University. No person, however famous, should be appointed to the University faculty with the understanding that he will do no teaching of any sort. Considerations regarding appointment should include the requirement that a candidate be willing to teach regularly and the expectation that he will teach effectively. Appointive bodies must bear in mind that teaching takes numerous forms. It occurs in lecture rooms, in small discussion groups, in research seminars, at the bedside in medical school, in laboratories, in reading courses, in the supervision of dissertations, and in the guidance of research assistants, postdoctoral students, and residents in hospitals. It should be borne in mind by appointive bodies seeking to assess the teaching accomplishments of candidates that no one is likely to be equally competent or outstanding in all the different forms of teaching.

The Committee regards the success of the student in learning his subject and in going on with it to an accomplishment of intellectual significance as the best test of effective teaching. Assessment of performance in teaching should not be unduly influenced by reports, accidentally or systematically obtained, about the popularity of a candidate with students or his "being an exciting teacher." Other evidence of teaching effectiveness such as arousing students' interest in a problem, stimulating them to work independently, clarifying certain problems in the student's mind, etc., must be sought by appointive bodies. The assessment of teaching should include accomplishments in curriculum planning, the design of particular courses, and other teaching activities which go beyond the direct face-to-face teaching of students. The teaching of introductory courses should count to a candidate's credit no less than the teaching of advanced courses. (The responsibility of teaching an elementary course should be recognized by reduced teaching schedules as compensation.)

There should be no appointment in which the appointed person is expected to spend most of his time on classroom teaching.

C. CONTRIBUTION TO THE INTELLECTUAL COMMUNITY

The University is not just an aggregate of individuals performing research or a collection of teachers instructing students at various levels and in various fields. It is an institution which provides the services, auxiliary services, and facilities for research and teaching. The University must be administered and it must have financial resources to enable its academic staff to perform the functions for which they have been appointed.

In addition to being an institution with an administration and financial resources which provide the framework and facilities for research and teaching by academic staff members and students, it is also an intellectual community and a constellation of overlapping intellectual subcommunities built around, but not bounded by, committees and schools. It is an intellectual community in which interaction is about intellectual matters. The contribution which a member of the academic staff makes to the work of his colleagues and students by his own work, by his conversation in informal situations and by his criticizing and reading of their manuscripts, by his discussion of their research and of problems in their own and related fields is of great importance in creating and maintaining the intellectual quality of the University. He also contributes through his role in devising and revising courses of study (curricula) and other activities which go beyond his own teaching.

To what extent should these contributions be considered by appointive bodies?

First, regarding administration, members of the academic staff are not appointed to fill administrative roles. The fact that a candidate for appointment has been an excellent dean or is a good "committee man" or willingly serves on departmental committees or has been or might be an excellent department chairman adds to the merit of a member of the academic staff. But it is a "gift of grace" and it is not pertinent to discussions about appointments, which must concentrate on intellectual performance, actual and prospective.

Although in principle younger members of the academic staff should be enabled to serve on committees and perform departmental duties other than their teaching and research, the decision regarding their reappointment or promotion should not be affected by their having or not having done so. The performance of some of these departmental chores often being at the expense of research, an appointments policy which accords importance to accomplishments of this sort might be injurious to the young staff member's development as a scholar or scientist.

Universities require financial resources to support research, teaching, and administration of the university. Nonetheless, the capacity or incapacity of a candidate to attract financial resources or to "bring them with him" should not be a criterion for appointment. The acquisition of financial resources should be a task of the administration and a derivative function of the distinguished scientific or scholarly accomplishments and capacities of the members of the University faculty. If this rule is not observed, the University will be in danger of becoming an aggregate of affluent mediocrities.

The intellectual contribution of the academic staff member to his colleagues and students is a different matter. It is partly a function of his research and teaching accomplishments, but it also goes far beyond them. If a candidate is known to greatly stimulate his colleagues and students by his conversation and his criticism of their work, so that their individual performances are thereby improved, this should weigh in the consideration of a candidate for appointment.

Influence on the intellectual life of the University as an institution can be negative as well as positive. A member of the academic staff might be an impediment to the University's performance of its intellectual functions, quite apart from his own performance as a research worker and teacher.

It should go without saying, therefore, that all appointees to the academic staff of the University should possess the requisite "academic citizenship." By this the Committee means that appointive bodies are entitled to expect that persons whom they appoint to the academic staff will contribute what they can to the intellectual life of the University through their research, teaching, and intellectual intercourse in the University, and that they will abstain from deliberate disruption of the regular operations of the University.

The University must operate as an institution in order for its individual members to pursue their research and teaching. Deliberate obstruction of the work of the University through participation in disruptive activities cannot claim the protection of academic freedom, which is the freedom of the individual to investigate, publish, and teach in accordance with his intellectual convictions. Indeed, the only connection between disruptive actions within the University and academic freedom is that the disruptive actions interfere with the very action which academic freedom is intended to protect. Appointive committees, concerned with the maintenance or improvement of the intellectual quality of research and teaching in the University, must expect that those whom they appoint will enjoy the protection of academic freedom and that they will also be the guardians of that freedom. It is pertinent at this point to affirm what was said above about the irrelevance of political or religious beliefs and affiliations to decisions regarding appointment.

D. SERVICES
   1. University Services
   A. Services Integral to Research and Training Outside Medicine

There are various kinds of services performed by members of the University. The first of these is the service which is indispensable for the performance of the central functions of the University in research and training. For example, faculty members in the physical sciences often require the collaboration of engineers for the conduct of their research. Such persons are normally highly qualified and could hold senior posts in engineering faculties or in industry. Their contribution is integral to research and although not members of the faculty they must therefore be accorded emoluments and privileges comparable to members of the University faculty of similar accomplishments and professional standing. Similarly, the training of social workers requires that supervisors be provided for their training in field work. Those performing these services are not defined by the University *Statutes* as members of the University faculty.[7]

B. Health Care and the Medical School

University service functions in the medical realm are those which do not *ipso facto* serve the primary functions of the University, viz., research and teaching. They include the provision of health care by the medical school to both the community at large and the student body. The staff who deliver these services are University faculty members in clinical departments, other academic personnel,[8] and perhaps additional persons not specified in the *Statutes*.

It must be emphasized that though delivery of health care may be solely a service function (as in student and employee health clinics), more frequently it is an integral part of the University as an academic institution. It is such when it involves the teaching and training of medical students, interns, residents, and fellows. Of fundamental importance is the fact that teaching and care at the bedside on the one hand and medical research on the other are mutually interdependent and continuous activities, both of which provide intellectual tasks of the highest order. The commitments of members of the University faculty in the clinical departments (unlike those of members of the faculty in the basic medical and biological sciences) are therefore threefold. The training of outstanding physicians requires that faculty members deliver the best of medical care in addition to their research and teaching activities. For many reasons, it is practically impossible to ensure that every appointment in clinical departments reflects a similarly balanced excellence in all three areas. Thus, appointments to various academic faculty ranks in the clinical disciplines usually embrace a wide range of personnel, ranging from research workers of acknowledged excellence whose contributions to patient care may be outstanding, good, or slight; physicians whose respective contributions are equally meritorious but not of the very first rank; and clinicians whose dedication to research is modest. some clinical departments also appoint a relatively small number of distinguished investigators who may or may not have a medical degree and who do not participate at all in clinical care.

The Committee believes that a great university medical school rapidly loses its eminence if it ceases to have a considerable number of outstanding investigators on the faculty of its clinical departments. Nevertheless, a medical school which cannot provide excellent care to the patients in its wards and clinics will produce only poor physicians and will fail to attract students, interns, and residents of high intellectual potentiality.

Physicians engaged in purely clinical work, who make no serious contributions to research or teaching, should under no circumstances be given any form of faculty rank or have any formal voice in recommendations for academic appointments. Many such clinicians who are not members of the University faculty are at present given the title of "research associate."[9] This term may be a misnomer in as much as these persons are not engaged in research and the title is also used as an additional designation for bona fide faculty members who hold joint appointments in two or more departments. The title of "clinical associate" might better describe persons involved in purely clinical service functions.

In situations where the financial competitiveness of private (or nonacademic) medicine has helped to deplete the academic pool of a clinical department, its resuscitation should depend more on attractive competitive stipends than on lowering the standards for academic appointments.

C. Concluding Observations on University Services

The likelihood of appointments for purely "service" purposes is increased whenever the University undertakes, for whatever reason, the extension of services not related to its research and teaching functions. Such enterprises by definition require expertise and performance of a different kind from those expected of regular faculty members, and appointments to meet such needs should never be appointments to the faculty (as defined by the University *Statutes*). Decisions to extend medical and other services which do not involve either teaching or research or both should be made in the awareness that whatever persons are appointed will not be granted the status of members of the University faculty.

2. External Services[10]
A. Public Services

There is a second type of service in which members of the academic staff become involved. This is public service, i.e., service for the federal, state, and municipal governments and for civic and voluntary associations. To what extent should appointive bodies consider accomplishments in such services as qualifications for appointment? The Committee is of the view that such services should not be considered as qualifications for academic appointment unless the service has a significant intellectual or research component. Thus, membership in a governmental body which does not perform research or make decisions regarding the promotion of research should not be regarded as a qualification for appointment. Membership in an advisory body which organizes, supports, and oversees research should be regarded as a positive qualification. Proximity to the design and execution of the research program and its quality must be taken into account.

Incumbency in elective or political office, whether it be the presidency of the United States or the prime ministry of a country, should not be regarded as a qualification for appointment to the academic staff of the University.

Participation in the "delivery" of services for the non-University community should be considered in decisions regarding academic appointment only when there is an increment to knowledge or a valuable function in instruction or training arising from the "delivery." Certain of these "deliveries" are undertaken as part of the "public relations" of the University or because government or civic bodies have not taken the initiative or responsibility which are properly theirs.

Nothing in the foregoing paragraphs should be interpreted as a judgment on the merit of the various public services or the appropriateness of their performance by members of the academic staff in their capacity as citizens. On the contrary, such services are often very important for society—local, national, and international. They must not, however, be counted as qualifications for academic appointment.

B. Academic Services

Among the service activities sometimes performed by members of the academic staff are those performed on behalf of learned and scientific societies which the Committee designates as "academic services." A threefold distinction can be made between (1) honorific services, e.g., presidency of a learned or scientific society; (2) intellectual services, such as editorship of a learned or scientific journal; and (3) administrative services, e.g., secretaryship of a learned or scientific society.

The first is a distinction conferred on persons who by their research have made and are making valuable contributions to their subjects. In most instances, such honorific offices represent a confirmation of the major criteria of academic appointment, namely distinction in research, and they may therefore be taken into positive account by appointive bodies.

The second, the editorship of a learned or scientific journal, is a contribution to the intellectual community in a particular discipline beyond the confines of the University. It is a contribution to the maintenance of standards of excellence in the discipline. It too should be taken into positive account by appointive bodies. Membership on advisory panels, e.g., National Institutes of Health (NIH) "study sections," is an intellectual service; it is similar to editorship of a learned or scientific journal and is a contribution to the national and international learned and scientific communities. It should, accordingly, be taken into positive account by appointive bodies.

The third academic service, the secretaryship or a similar administrative function on behalf of a learned or scientific society, on the other hand, is a time-consuming activity which does not entail contributions to teaching or research; this type of service should not be taken into positive account by appointive bodies.

C. Private Services

Consultative services for private industry are admissible as considerations in academic appointments only if they entail an enhancement of the scientific accomplishments of the person involved. This is the aspect which should concern appointive bodies.

IV. Conclusion

The positive task of appointive bodies, i.e., the appointment of persons of the highest abilities, has been the main focus of attention in this report. There are, however, also negative tasks; these are the refusal to make appointments. These negative tasks fall under three headings. The first is relatively simple; it is to refuse to make appointments when there are no available candidates of sufficiently high quality. The only excuse for appointing a candidate of acknowledgedly undistinguished qualifications is that certain necessary teaching must be done if students are to be prepared for their degrees. This necessity can be met by the expedient, referred to in the body of the report, of explicitly temporary appointments for particular teaching tasks. The irregular situation should be under constant review so that it can be restored to a regular condition through appointments of the proper quality.

Where there is no particular teaching task of great urgency, in situations where there are no candidates of sufficiently high quality, actual or prospective, no appointments should be made. It is better for the University to allow a field to lie fallow than to allow it to be poorly cultivated. Appointments should not be made just because there is a list of candidates and funds to pay their salaries.

Appointive bodies have a second negative function, and this is to exercise a stern scrutiny over expansion. This responsibility, of course, they cannot exercise alone; they depend heavily here on the support and cooperation of the dean of the relevant division, the provost, and the president of the University.

Great care must be exercised in expanding the staff in established fields or in reaching into new fields of academic work. One of the great advantages of the University of Chicago in the present situation of universities in the world is that it is relatively small. There are many things which universities do, some of which are useful and admirable, but which need not be done by the University of Chicago. There is a great temptation, both when financial support is plenteous and when it is scarce, to take on new members, new fields of study and research, and new service functions because financial support is available. Some of these might be properly done by the University of Chicago where the University has a tradition which would enable them to be very well done or where there are clear and important intellectual and institutional benefits to be obtained from doing them.

But to allow expansion and new appointments simply because financial resources are available to support them would be an error which would be wasteful of resources and damaging to the University.

The judicious performance of this negative task must not, however, be permitted to prevent the taking up of important new fields of study and research about which there are genuine and well-based intellectual convictions in the University and outstanding intellectual capacities to do them outstandingly well. Even where a field is intellectually important, the University, and this also means appointive bodies, should not venture into them simply because other outstanding universities are working in them. The expansion into the important new field should be undertaken only if appointments at a high level of quality can be made to provide the necessary staff.

There is a third negative function, already referred to in the body of this report.

This is the problem of dealing with fields in decline because the subject has become exhausted within the country or in the world at large or because not enough young persons of sufficient potentiality for distinguished accomplishment wish to enter them.

The last three tasks are negative only in the sense that they involve the refusal to make appointments when the quality of the candidates is not sufficiently high. In fact, however, these negative functions, if properly performed, are as positive in their outcome as the more obviously positive tasks. It is indeed only if equal attention is paid to both—i.e., to the need for adamant refusal to be tempted into making appointments just because appointments can be made, as well as to the firm insistence on appointing candidates of actually or potentially great merit—that the University of Chicago will be what it ought to be. Only by an undeviating adherence to the criteria set forth in this report can the University of Chicago maintain and enhance its reputation among the universities of the world as a university of the first rank in certain fields, regain that position in others in which it has declined, and open up important new fields which no other universities have yet entered.

V. A Later Elaboration on Political Criteria

On 2 December 1971, the Committee on the Criteria of Academic Appointment was asked by President Levi to reconvene so that it could elaborate its views on political criteria in decisions regarding academic appointment, reappointment, and promotion.

In the *Report of the Committee on the Criteria of Academic Appointment* we said: "There must be no consideration of sex, ethnic or national characteristics, or political or religious beliefs or affiliations in any decision regarding appointment, promotion or reappointment at any level of the academic staff" (see "The Application of Criteria," p. 000). Further on in the Report, in connection with "academic citizenship," we affirmed the earlier statement about "the irrelevance of political or religious beliefs and affiliations to decisions regarding appointments" (see "Contribution to the Intellectual Community," p. 000).

We now wish to elaborate the foregoing statements as follows:

In discussions and decisions regarding appointments, promotions, and reappointments, appointive bodies should concentrate their consideration of any candidate on his qualifications as a research worker, teacher, and member of the academic community. The candidate's past or current conduct should be considered only insofar as it conveys information relative to the assessment of his excellence as an investigator, the quality of the publications which he lays before the academic community, the fruitfulness of his teaching and the steadfastness of his adherence to the highest standards of intellectual performance, professional probity, and the humanity and mutual tolerance which must prevail among scholars.

There are, accordingly, certain matters which when they do not unambiguously and demonstrably bear on the application of the foregoing criteria, must be studiously avoided in discussions about academic appointment. These matters include a candidate's past and current associations and the objectives of his past or current employer, the sources of the funds which support his research and the uses to which third parties might or have actually put its results independently of his desires. It behooves all members of the University of Chicago to do all they can to ensure that the standards set forth above are strictly observed in discussions and decisions regarding academic appointments.

Committee

Edward Shils, *Chairman*
Distinguished Service Professor of Sociology and in the Committee on
   Social Thought

S. Chandrasekhar
Morton D. Hull Distinguished Service Professor of Astronomy and
   Physics

Dr. Roderick Childers
Associate Professor of Medicine

John Hope Franklin
John Matthews Manly Distinguished Service Professor of History

Arthur Friedman
Distinguished Service Professor of English

Jacob W. Getzels
R. Wendell Harrison Distinguished Service Professor of Education
and Psychology

Harry G. Johnson
Professor of Economics

Saunders Mac Lane
Max Mason Distinguished Service Professor of Mathematics

Edward Rosenheim, Secretary
Professor of English

John Simpson
Edward L. Ryerson Distinguished Service Professor of Physics

Lorna P. Straus
Assistant Professor of Anatomy and Biology

H. G. Williams-Ashman
Professor of Biochemistry and in the Ben May Laboratory for Cancer
Research

On Protest and Dissent

*A report by a University of Chicago
ad hoc faculty committee*

JANUARY 13, 2014

In 2010, eighteen-year-old Damian Turner was shot very close to the University. The world-class University of Chicago Medical Center, however, did not have a Level 1 adult trauma center, and Turner died on the way to the Northwestern Memorial Hospital, over seven miles away, in downtown Chicago. This led to young community activists launching a campaign to bring a trauma center to the University, which had closed the prior center in the 1980s for lack of profitability. The campaign involved sit-ins and protests, including occupation of parts of the hospital and Levi Hall, but the University resisted the pressure for some time. In 2013, President Zimmer appointed a committee, under the chairmanship of legal scholar David Strauss, to develop principles on how protest ought to be handled. The ensuing report clarifies that within the University context of robust discussion and debate, protest and dissent are to be "affirmatively welcomed." Their absence would be cause for concern. The University of Chicago reopened a Level 1 adult trauma center in May 2018.

I. Background

The Provost established this committee in Winter Quarter, 2013. His charge to the Committee is reproduced in Appendix I [omitted here].

The committee was established in the aftermath of demonstrations at the Center for Care and Discovery that led to arrests and disciplinary actions against demonstrators and allegations of misconduct against the University of Chicago Police Department. The events surrounding those demonstrations were addressed by a separate investigation and report, and those specific events are not the subject of this Committee's work. The Provost directed us instead to make recommendations about the principles that should govern protests and demonstrations on campus in the future.

In addition to charging the Committee to make general recommendations about policies and practices related to dissent, the Provost identified three specific issues. First, he asked us to consider whether protests and demonstrations at especially sensitive University facilities, such as health care and research facilities, should be treated differently from demonstrations at other University buildings. Second, he asked how rules and guidelines about protests and demonstrations should apply when the group engaged in the demonstration includes both people affiliated with the University and people, perhaps from nearby communities, who do not have a University affiliation.

Third, he asked what expectations there should be about communications among protesters, University police, and other University officials and staff members, and what responsibilities those groups should have toward each other.

The Committee met with University administrators, students, and representatives of the Hyde Park community. Members of the Committee invited comments from colleagues, and the Committee held an open meeting for the entire University community on 13 May 2013. A list of these various meetings is Appendix II [omitted here]. In addition, the Committee established an email address to which any interested person could send comments.

This report reflects the unanimous view of the members of the Committee. We will first offer some general thoughts about the relationship of protest, dissent, and demonstrations to the University's mission. Then we will make some observations on the University's existing policies governing protest and dissent and some specific recommendations.

II. General Principles

In our view, dissent and protest are integral to the life of the University. Dissent and protest should be affirmatively welcomed, not merely tolerated, by the University. Especially in a university community, the absence of dissent and protest—not its presence—is a cause for concern. The passionate expression of non-conforming ideas is both a cause and an effect of the intellectual climate that defines this University in particular. In addition, dissent and protest—and public demonstrations by groups and individuals—play a role in the University's educational mission: being a member of an educational community that values dissent and protest is, in part, how people develop as citizens of a democracy.

But maintaining this kind of university community imposes obligations of mutual respect on everyone involved. University administrators have a responsibility to act with restraint and flexibility and not to insist on the enforcement of rules for its own sake. Beyond that, University administrators have an obligation to listen and to engage: to recognize the concerns of dissenters and to address those concerns to the extent they can.

People engaged in protests and demonstrations have reciprocal obligations of respect and constructive engagement. They have a responsibility not to jeopardize the University's ability to meet its commitments and obligations. A university like ours is a complex institution that is engaged in a wide range of activities, including some highly sensitive activities the disruption of which would have very harmful consequences for members of the University community. Protesters have a responsibility to recognize that and to act accordingly.

III. Current Policies

The University's existing policies on dissent and protest (attached as Appendix III) [omitted here] are, for the most part, less specific than those of many comparable universities. This University does not, for example, have a detailed code of conduct that regulates demonstrations and other activities related to protest. Instead, the University's policies rely on more general standards.

We believe this is a virtue, and we do not recommend a substantial revision of the University's existing written policies. The existing policies allow for flexibility and for the exercise of discretion, and that is how it should be. We will suggest some relatively minor revisions in the next part of this report.

The existing policies contemplate that demonstrations will be planned in advance, with cooperation between University administrators and protesters; that is one of the reasons that our policies can be flexible rather than rule-bound. There is a record of successful cooperation in the past: protesters have been able to engage in the kinds of demonstrations they wanted, without excessive disruption of University activities. This kind of antecedent cooperation between protesters and University administrators is very important, and we believe the organizers of protests have a responsibility to engage in this process. It enables the University not just to permit but to welcome and facilitate and, if necessary, to protect the people demonstrating. That is the attitude University administrators should take toward protest, and it is the attitude they have expressed in their meetings with us.

At the same time, spontaneous demonstrations that have not been previously coordinated with the University cannot, and should not, be ruled out. The University should, to the maximum extent it can, adopt the same approach of restraint when spontaneous demonstrations happen; if possible, the University should facilitate those protests as well. But people engaged in a spontaneous demonstration have an absolute obligation to respect the University's legitimate interests in protecting its facilities and its operations. The University has not just the right but the responsibility to protect those interests if they are jeopardized.

IV. Specific Recommendations

1. Whenever possible, problems that arise in connection with protest activity should be handled with a minimum of police involve-

ON PROTEST AND DISSENT   203

ment. If this requires that additional resources be devoted to the Dean-on-Call program, then we recommend that those resources be provided.

In addition, a decision that the University Police be called in should be made, if at all possible, by high-ranking University officials. University Police should be trained in techniques adapted to providing the necessary security during demonstrations in order to protect protesters and bystanders as well as the University's vital interests. Our understanding is that policies along these lines have been implemented, or are being implemented, already.

2. The University is entitled to impose strict limits on protest activity that threatens especially sensitive facilities and to enforce those limits if they are breached. We do not think it is possible to specify, acontextually, what these limits might be. That may depend on the specific uses being made of a facility, on the nature of the protest activity that is contemplated, and on other factors. The University should, however, give clear notice of the limits it is imposing. It should accommodate protest activity to the extent possible, and it should, as always, act with restraint to the extent compatible with the protection of its vital interests.

3. The University should expect that members of the community outside the University will engage in protest near or on University property, often in concert with members of the University community. The University should minimize differences in treatment between University affiliates and non-affiliates, in order to avoid seeming to adopt an unwelcoming attitude toward members of the outside community.

Having said that, however, the University has special responsibilities toward members of the University community. The University can also insist on certain standards of behavior (and impose discipline accordingly) in its relationship with members of the University community. For those reasons, in some circumstances it will be entirely appropriate for the University to treat members of its community differently from people who are not members of the University community.

4. In dealing with matters that might give rise to protests, the University should be alert to the benefits of collaborating with representatives of the neighboring communities and other stakeholders. Particularly when these matters affect people who are not affiliated with the University, representatives of other communities can help the University communicate the reasons for its decisions in a more effective way. Our neighboring communities, by identifying and articulating their interests, can also help protect against the exploitation of members of the University community by groups that have an agenda that is not compatible with the University's values or with the interests of either the University or its neighbors.

5. Because an atmosphere that welcomes protest and dissent is, as we have said, a component of the University's educational mission, the University should consider introducing students more explicitly to the specific policies governing protest and dissent and, perhaps more importantly, to the University's general principles about protest and dissent. This could take place during orientation; it should also be a subject addressed with the leadership of student groups on an ongoing basis, as appropriate.

6. The University's policies should, to the extent possible, make clear what discipline will be imposed for violations of University rules. In that connection, two aspects of the University's policies may warrant revision. The University's written policies currently provide for an all-University disciplinary system that, we understand, has not been used for decades and that should be re-evaluated.

More directly relevant to protest and dissent, we note that the University's statutes appear to provide that discipline can be imposed for "[c]onduct . . . disruptive of the operations of the University." Statute 21, Statutes of the University of Chicago (2013). This prohibition, taken literally, is too broad. Vocal protest, and demonstrations in particular, are by their nature disruptive to some degree.

There is a more specific definition of disruption in legislation enacted by the Council of the University Senate (Legislation enacted

May 12, 1970; amended June 8, 1976). That definition (reproduced, along with Statute 21, in Appendix IV) [omitted here] is more appropriately limited, especially if it is applied—as it should be—with a proper understanding of the role of protest activity in the University community and with a recognition that protest activity will often cause incidental disruption. Such incidental disruption should not be regarded as a violation of University policy.

David A. Strauss, *Committee Chair*
Gerald Ratner Distinguished Service Professor of Law

Emilio Kourí
Professor, Departments of History and Romance Languages and
    Literatures and the College

Stacy Lindau
Associate Professor, Department of Obstetrics and Gynecology

Emil J. Martinec
Professor, Department of Physics, the Enrico Fermi Institute, and the
    College

Everett E. Vokes
John E. Ultmann Professor, Department of Medicine

Christopher Woods
Associate Professor, Oriental Institute, Department of Near Eastern
    Languages and Civilizations, and the College

Ingrid Gould, Staff to Committee
Associate Provost for Faculty and Student Affairs

On Freedom of Expression

A report by a University of Chicago faculty committee

2015

One of President Zimmer's most celebrated acts in service of free expression was the appointment of the Committee on Freedom of Expression, under the chairmanship of legal scholar Geoffrey R. Stone. The result, known locally as the Stone report, has been widely cited and adopted by other institutions of higher education. Purdue University president Mitch Daniels dubbed the content "the Chicago Principles," and to this date they mark a touchstone for thinking about the role of free expression in a university setting. Interestingly, Stone and other members of the committee have described their surprise that the report had such uptake, as it was only intended as an internal statement of Chicago values and practices.

The Committee on Freedom of Expression at the University of Chicago was appointed in July 2014 by President Robert J. Zimmer and Provost Eric D. Isaacs "in light of recent events nationwide that have tested institutional commitments to free and open discourse." The Committee's charge was to draft a statement "articulating the University's overarching commitment to free, robust, and uninhibited debate and deliberation among all members of the University's community."

The Committee has carefully reviewed the University's history, examined events at other institutions, and consulted a broad range of individuals both inside and outside the University. This statement reflects the long-standing and distinctive values of the

University of Chicago and affirms the importance of maintaining and, indeed, celebrating those values for the future.

From its very founding, the University of Chicago has dedicated itself to the preservation and celebration of the freedom of expression as an essential element of the University's culture. In 1902, in his address marking the University's decennial, President William Rainey Harper declared that "the principle of complete freedom of speech on all subjects has from the beginning been regarded as fundamental in the University of Chicago" and that "this principle can neither now nor at any future time be called in question."

Thirty years later, a student organization invited William Z. Foster, the Communist Party's candidate for President, to lecture on campus. This triggered a storm of protest from critics both on and off campus. To those who condemned the University for allowing the event, President Robert M. Hutchins responded that "our students ... should have freedom to discuss any problem that presents itself." He insisted that the "cure" for ideas we oppose "lies through open discussion rather than through inhibition." On a later occasion, Hutchins added that "free inquiry is indispensable to the good life, that universities exist for the sake of such inquiry, [and] that without it they cease to be universities."

In 1968, at another time of great turmoil in universities, President Edward H. Levi, in his inaugural address, celebrated "those virtues which from the beginning and until now have characterized our institution." Central to the values of the University of Chicago, Levi explained, is a profound commitment to "freedom of inquiry." This freedom, he proclaimed, "is our inheritance."

More recently, President Hanna Holborn Gray observed that "education should not be intended to make people comfortable, it is meant to make them think. Universities should be expected to provide the conditions within which hard thought, and therefore strong disagreement, independent judgment, and the questioning of stubborn assumptions, can flourish in an environment of the greatest freedom."

The words of Harper, Hutchins, Levi, and Gray capture both the spirit and the promise of the University of Chicago. Because the University is committed to free and open inquiry in all matters, it guarantees all members of the University community the broadest possible latitude to speak, write, listen, challenge, and learn. Except insofar as limitations on that freedom are necessary to the functioning of the University, the University of Chicago fully respects and supports the freedom of all members of the University community "to discuss any problem that presents itself."

Of course, the ideas of different members of the University community will often and quite naturally conflict. But it is not the proper role of the University to attempt to shield individuals from ideas and opinions they find unwelcome, disagreeable, or even deeply offensive. Although the University greatly values civility, and although all members of the University community share in the responsibility for maintaining a climate of mutual respect, concerns about civility and mutual respect can never be used as a justification for closing off discussion of ideas, however offensive or disagreeable those ideas may be to some members of our community.

The freedom to debate and discuss the merits of competing ideas does not, of course, mean that individuals may say whatever they wish, wherever they wish. The University may restrict expression that violates the law, that falsely defames a specific individual, that constitutes a genuine threat or harassment, that unjustifiably invades substantial privacy or confidentiality interests, or that is otherwise directly incompatible with the functioning of the University. In addition, the University may reasonably regulate the time, place, and manner of expression to ensure that it does not disrupt the ordinary activities of the University. But these are narrow exceptions to the general principle of freedom of expression, and it is vitally important that these exceptions never be used in a manner that is inconsistent with the University's commitment to a completely free and open discussion of ideas.

In a word, the University's fundamental commitment is to the principle that debate or deliberation may not be suppressed because the ideas put forth are thought by some or even by most members of the University community to be offensive, unwise, immoral, or wrongheaded. It is for the individual members of the University community, not for the University as an institution, to make those judgments for themselves, and to act on those judgments not by seeking to suppress speech, but by openly and vigorously contesting the ideas that they oppose. Indeed, fostering the ability of members of the University community to engage in such debate and deliberation in an effective and responsible manner is an essential part of the University's educational mission.

As a corollary to the University's commitment to protect and promote free expression, members of the University community must also act in conformity with the principle of free expression. Although members of the University community are free to criticize and contest the views expressed on campus, and to criticize and contest speakers who are invited to express their views on campus, they may not obstruct or otherwise interfere with the freedom of others to express views they reject or even loathe. To this end, the University has a solemn responsibility not only to promote a lively and fearless freedom of debate and deliberation, but also to protect that freedom when others attempt to restrict it.

As Robert M. Hutchins observed, without a vibrant commitment to free and open inquiry, a university ceases to be a university. The University of Chicago's long-standing commitment to this principle lies at the very core of our University's greatness. That is our inheritance, and it is our promise to the future.

Geoffrey R. Stone, *Chair*
Edward H. Levi Distinguished Service Professor of Law

Marianne Bertrand
Chris P. Dialynas Distinguished Service Professor of Economics, Booth
    School of Business

Angela Olinto
Homer J. Livingston Professor, Department of Astronomy and
    Astrophysics, Enrico Fermi Institute, and the College

Mark Siegler
Lindy Bergman Distinguished Service Professor of Medicine and Surgery

David A. Strauss
Gerald Ratner Distinguished Service Professor of Law

Kenneth W. Warren
Fairfax M. Cone Distinguished Service Professor, Department of English
     and the College

Amanda Woodward
William S. Gray Professor, Department of Psychology and the College

On University Discipline for Disruptive Conduct

Revised final report of a University of Chicago faculty committee

JUNE 2, 2017

The disruptive protests around the trauma center conflict in the early 2010s, along with perceptions of inconsistent disciplinary processes and policies around the campus, led President Zimmer to appoint a third committee, under the chairmanship of legal scholar Randal Picker. The committee examined the existing rules and recommended changes, while also spelling out clear consequences for violations and centralizing the disciplinary process. One result has been the creation of a centralized process for determining when protest and dissent cross the line into disruption.

On June 2, 2016, the Provost of the University appointed [this faculty] committee to, among other tasks, "review and make recommendations about procedures for student disciplinary matters involving disruptive conduct including interference with freedom of inquiry or debate."[1] On February 20, 2017, the committee issued a preliminary report on these issues. After discussion and comment on campus and after a vote on May 23, 2017 by the Council of the University Senate approving Appendix V [omitted here] to this report, the committee issued this revised and final version of its report.

The University has considered the issues discussed here in two recent reports, the 2014 *Report of the Ad Hoc Committee on Protest and Dissent* and the 2015 *Report of the Committee on Freedom of Expression.*[2] The University's statutes establish the rules and procedures for addressing disruptive conduct at the University. "Disruptive conduct" is defined in Statute 21 of the University Statutes, and the Council of the University Senate is assigned in Statute 12.5.3.5 certain authority to establish rules implementing that statute. . . . The *Protest and Dissent Report* recommended changes to Statute 21, that later were adopted by the Council, and urged the University to re-evaluate the existing All-University Disciplinary System adopted in 1970, but not invoked since 1974. We undertook that re-evaluation as part of producing this Report.

The *Freedom of Expression Report* states that "the University's fundamental commitment is to the principle that debate or deliberation may not be suppressed because the ideas put forth are thought by some or even by most members of the University community to be offensive, unwise, immoral, or wrong-headed," while the *Protest and Dissent Report* emphasizes that "[d]issent and protest should be affirmatively welcomed, not merely tolerated, by the University." Our recommendations in this Report are informed by those two core University values.

Framing Principles

After reviewing the prior reports and having an extensive series of meetings with faculty, students, staff, members of the Hyde Park community and others, the Committee identified a set of key constructive principles for framing our recommendations:

1. The speech that takes place at the University is first and foremost determined by the faculty, other scholars and students present at the University.
2. Norms of respect, civility, openness and inclusion are essential to enable speech from everyone at the University. A restrictive, hostile,

unwelcoming climate will shrink expression, while a rich, friendly, inclusive climate will enable speech to thrive.

3. At the University, we share a free-speech commons, by which we mean the communal forum, shared by everyone who participates in the life of the University, in which free expression takes place and that is subject to certain reasonable rules if the commons is to continue to thrive.

4. The fundamental operating principle of the University free-speech commons is one of decentralization and local creation of expression supported by central authority to ensure that the University's free-speech values are upheld fully.

5. The University operates in this fashion because doing otherwise would be antithetical to the core idea that knowledge is best created by individual faculty members, other academic appointees, postdoctoral researchers and students.

6. Protesters are fully within their free-speech rights to counter and object to speech, as long as they are doing so without blocking or disrupting the free-speech rights of others.

7. Disruptive conduct may itself be a form of speech, but that does not mean that it is a protected form of speech. Like other forms of civil disobedience, disruptive conduct may lead to disciplinary consequences for those engaged in such conduct.

8. The benefits and burdens of a robust free-speech commons will not be distributed evenly, and the University itself can and does speak to address that fact when warranted.

Recommendations from the Committee

I. THE CURRENT ALL-UNIVERSITY DISCIPLINARY SYSTEM SHOULD BE REPLACED WITH A REVISED CENTRALIZED DISCIPLINARY SYSTEM.

Disruptive conduct is currently addressed in individual units outside of the All-University Disciplinary System. We recommend instead a centralized disciplinary process for disruptive conduct with the hope that doing so will provide greater consistency across cases. Consistent with that idea, we recommend lodging some administrative aspects of the proposed new structure with the Associate Dean of Students in the University for Disciplinary Affairs. We also recommend that resolution of disruptive conduct matters be handled by a voting committee of five individuals (three statutory faculty members, one student and one staff member) who will be drawn from a larger pool appointed by the Provost. We think it imprudent to propose a particular menu or algorithm of offenses and corresponding disciplinary responses. Given the statutory role played by the Council of the University Senate in Section 12.5.3.5 of the University Statutes, we propose a set of procedures in Appendix V.[3] Appendix V [omitted here] as attached hereto was approved by the Council of the University Senate on May 23, 2017.

2. AS IT SUPPORTS PROTEST AND DISSENT, THE UNIVERSITY SHOULD REVISE ITS PROCEDURES FOR EVENT MANAGEMENT TO REDUCE THE CHANCES THAT THOSE ENGAGED IN DISRUPTIVE CONDUCT CAN PREVENT OTHERS FROM SPEAKING OR BEING HEARD.

The University's existing approach to event management suffers from two defects: deans-on-call have not been given clear guidance on how to respond to disruptive conduct and they lack the authority to act decisively to protect free speech. We recommend that the University create free-speech deans-on-call with special training to deal with disruptive conduct, and we further recommend an advance-authorization structure to enable, if necessary, removal of disruptive individual(s) from events. The current rules, which often force deans-on-call to try to contact other administrators at the University in the middle of a free-speech disruption, are simply unworkable.

The committee recommends that the University provide greater clarity on the roles and responsibilities of hosts, speakers, audience members, event staff and the University Police at events to improve understanding of the University's commitment to free expression and clarify the consequences of disrupting the free-speech commons. This can be achieved by complementing the existing event-review process with more explicit audience guidelines, increased dean-on-call staffing at events, and more robust training for event staff. To ensure transparency for students and the broader University community, the audience guidelines for events, the role of the deans-on-call and UCPD, protocols for responding to disruptive conduct, and potential legal and disciplinary consequences of disruptive conduct should be readily available and accessible in the *Student Manual of University Policies and Regulations* and on a dedicated University website.[4]

3. THE UNIVERSITY SHOULD MODIFY ITS EXISTING APPROACH TO DISRUPTIVE CONDUCT BY INDIVIDUALS WHO ARE NOT CURRENTLY AFFILIATED WITH THE UNIVERSITY.

Consistent with the University's broad mission in research and education, the University generally welcomes individuals who are not currently affiliated with the University to participate in many of its activities. Individuals who come to the University have the same duty to preserve the free-speech commons and refrain from engaging in disruptive conduct. The Committee believes that the University should make every reasonable effort to treat unaffiliated individuals the same way it treats affiliated people in connection with disruptive conduct. The Committee recognizes, however that the University's ability to address disruptive conduct by unaffiliated people is more limited than the options available when addressing disruptive conduct by faculty and other scholars, students and staff.

When appropriate, unaffiliated individuals who engage in disruptive conduct can be barred from all or part of the University permanently or for discrete periods under standards and processes set forth in the University's No-Trespass (Ban) Policy. The Committee recognizes that, by design, the individuals charged with administering the No-Trespass (Ban) Policy are required to use reasoned judgment when deciding whether to bar an individual. The Committee recommends that those administering the policy strive to achieve consistency in treating like cases in a substantially similar fashion and tailor no-trespass directives to fit the circumstances, especially as related to the duration of the prohibition, as the Committee expects that a permanent bar will be a rarely used outcome.

4. THE UNIVERSITY NEEDS A MORE ROBUST PROGRAM OF EDUCATIONAL PROGRAMMING TO ENSURE THAT STUDENTS UNDERSTAND THE RIGHTS AND RESPONSIBILITIES OF PARTICIPATING IN THE FREE-SPEECH COMMONS AT THE UNIVERSITY.

The Committee recommends new, targeted measures for students and student organizations building on existing student-centered programs and resources. Because of its role in shaping the co-curricular experience at the University, the Committee suggests that the Office of Campus and Student Life (CSL) serve a coordinating function in the development and implementation of educational and training efforts in collaboration with the area deans of students. To every extent possible, faculty should be invited to provide advice and participate in the development and execution of these various efforts. The Committee has had extensive discussions regarding possible education programs to implement this recommendation and has conveyed those to CSL. . . .

. . . This is the third University report in the last four years addressing the topic of freedom of expression at the University. That fact reflects both the importance of these issues and the genuine difficulties associated with creating and maintaining a space open to speech, including speech in protest of other speech. The Committee agreed to this undertaking precisely because of its importance to the University, and we firmly hope and believe that the recommendations set forth in this report will help to accomplish that end.

Randal C. Picker, *Committee Chair*
Daniel Abebe
Kerwin Charles
Jane Dailey

Karen Kim

Jeanne Marsh

Carole Ober

Michele Rasmussen

Christopher Wild

Ingrid Gould, *staff*

Ted Stamatakos, *staff*

Notes

Introduction

1   Alasdair MacIntyre, *After Virtue: A Study in Moral Theory* (Notre Dame, IN: University of Notre Dame Press, 2007), 222.

2   Janel Mueller, "Aims of Education Address 1994: Coeducation at Chicago; Whose Aims?," https://college.uchicago.edu/student-life/aims-education-address-1994 -janel-mueller.

3   Harper to Rockefeller, September 22, 1890, University of Chicago Founders' Correspondence, Box 1, folder 11, quoted in John W. Boyer, *The University of Chicago: A History* (Chicago: University of Chicago Press, 2015), 73.

4   William Rainey Harper, "The University and Democracy," Charter Day address, 1899, University of California. In Harper, *The Trend in Higher Education* (Chicago, 1905), 8.

5   *University of Chicago Official Bulletin*, 1891–1892, description of proposed University organization and academic programs, Hanna Holborn Gray Special Collections Research Center, Regenstein Library, University of Chicago.

6   Harper, "The University and Democracy," 8. And further, "The three birth-marks of a university are, therefore, self-government, freedom from ecclesiastical control, and the right of free utterance. And these certainly give it the right to proclaim itself an institution of the people, an institution born of the democratic spirit" (4).

7   Professor Paul Shorey developed the motto by combining lines from Alfred Tennyson's *In Memoriam A. H. H.* and the sixth book of Virgil's *Aeneid*. David Allen Robertson, "The Phoenix and the Book," *University of Chicago Magazine*, June 1912.

8   Robertson, "The Phoenix and the Book," 247–48. The reference, of course, is to the Great Chicago Fire of 1871, an inferno that leveled over three square miles of the young metropolis. The lesser-known reference is to the Old University of Chicago, founded in 1856, which financial hardship rendered inactive by the 1880s.

9   Harper, "The University and Democracy," 4.

10   Harper, 12.

11   John W. Boyer, *Academic Freedom and the Modern University: The Experience of the University of Chicago* (Chicago: The College of the University of Chicago, 2016), 14–20.

12   Of course, if taken as a normative proscription that "complete freedom of speech on all subjects" can "neither now nor at any time be called in question," the two principles are contradictory. An alternative reading of the second principle is that it is not normative, but descriptive. On that understanding, the very act of calling the foundational principle of complete freedom of speech into question is itself an exercise of complete freedom of speech—and so it is simply not possible to call the principle into question without exemplifying the very principle one may seek to refute.

13   "Academic Freedom," *Educational Review* 23 (January–May 1902): 1–14. Dewey's wife, Alice, was the principal of the University's Laboratory School, founded by Dewey in 1896. Disputes over the operation of the Laboratory School led Dewey to leave the University to move to Columbia in 1904. See John Dykhuizen, "John Dewey in Chicago: Some Biographical Notes," *Journal of the History of Philosophy* 3, no. 2 (October 1965): 217–33.

14   Dewey, "Academic Freedom," 10.

15   Minutes of the Council of the University Senate, October 17, 1950, 4:21, Office of the Secretary of the Faculties, University of Chicago. We are indebted to John Boyer for identifying this statement and pointing it out to us.

16   Regents of the University of California v. Bakke, 438 U.S. 265, 314 (1978). "The interest of diversity is compelling in the context of a university's admissions program."

17   Tom Ginsburg, "A Constitutional Perspective on Institutional Neutrality," in *Revisiting the Kalven Report: The University's Role in Social and Political Action*, ed. Keith E. Whittington and John Tomasi (Baltimore: Johns Hopkins University Press, forthcoming).

18   See, for example, Jennifer Roth, "The Uses and Abuses of the Kalven Report," *Chronicle of Higher Education*, October 24, 2023; Jeffrey Flier, "Now Is the Time for Administrators to Embrace Neutrality," *Chronicle of Higher Education*, October 13, 2023; and "The Wisdom of the University of Chicago's 'Kalven Report,'" FIRE, October 12, 2023, https://www.thefire.org/news/wisdom-university-chicagos-kalven -report.

19   Paul Alivisatos, "The Enormous Gifts and Great Responsibilities of the Chicago Principles for Members of our Community," message to the University of Chicago community, November 1, 2023, https://president.uchicago.edu/from-the-president /messages/231101-enormous-gifts-and-great-responsibilities.

20   It is available on the College website, at https://college.uchicago.edu/student-life /aims-education.

21   Clifford Ando, "All Amazing, All Unequal: Response to John W. Boyer on the State of the University's Finances," *Chicago Maroon*, December 21, 2023.

22   Emily J. Levine, *Allies and Rivals: German-American Exchange and the Rise of the Modern Research University* (Chicago: University of Chicago Press, 2021), 92.

23   See Danielle Allen's exhibit text from *Integrating the Life of the Mind: African Americans at the University of Chicago, 1870–1940*, Hanna Holborn Gray Special

Collections Research Center, September 1, 2008–February 28, 2009, available at https://www.lib.uchicago.edu/collex/exhibits/integrating-life-mind/.

24   Tom Ginsburg, "Conversation and Democracy," 2023 convocation address; video available at https://news.uchicago.edu/videos/2023-convocation-faculty-speaker-prof-tom-ginsburg.

25   Edward H. Levi, inaugural convocation address, November 14, 1968.

Dewey, "Academic Freedom"

1   See the *University Record*, 5, no. 42 (1901): 377.

Hutchins, "What Is a University?"

1   Hanna Holborn Gray, *Searching for Utopia: Universities and Their Histories* (Berkeley: University of California Press, 2012), 10.

Hutchins, "Broyles Commission Testimony"

1   John W. Boyer, *The University of Chicago: A History* (Chicago: University of Chicago Press, 2015), 306, citing Harry Ashmore interview by George Dell of May 25, 1976, Robert M. Hutchins and Associates, Oral History Interviews, Box 1, folder 3.

Levi, "Unrest and the Universities"

1   From the 21st Century King James Version of the Bible: "Where there is no vision, the people perish."

"On the University's Role in Political and Social Action"

1   White to Kalven, quoted in Mariana Fang, "Born amidst '60s Student Protests, Kalven Report Remains Controversial," *Chicago Maroon*, February 21, 2013, https://

chicagomaroon.com/16703/news/born-amidst-60s-student-protests-kalven
-report-remains-controversial/.

2   Jamie Kalven, "Unfinished Business of the Kalven Report," *Chicago Maroon*,
November 28, 2006. https://chicagomaroon.com/7464/viewpoints/op-ed
/unfinished-business-of-the-kalven-report/.

"On the Criteria of Academic Appointment"

1   In view of the invidious implications of the use of the masculine pronoun in all cases,
it should be clearly understood from the beginning that where that pronoun is used,
the reader of this report should understand it to refer to both sexes. Henry James once
said, "When I say 'Oxford,' I mean 'Oxford and Cambridge.'" We are, *mutatis mutandis*, in
the same position. When the term *department* alone is used, it should be understood to
refer to department, committee, institute, and school. When *appointment* alone is used,
it should be understood, unless it is otherwise clear from the context, that this means
appointment, promotion, retention, or extension. When we speak of "senior members"
of the University faculty, we mean those on permanent appointment; when we speak
of "junior members," we mean those not on permanent appointment. The University of
Chicago is generally referred to in the text as "the University."

2   The criteria for academic appointments sometimes are distorted or degraded by
pressures from the faculty or administration as a result of the need for special talent
to carry out supporting services of the University or to fulfill a commitment made by
the University to perform certain services.

3   [Footnote regarding University statutes omitted.]

4   Not necessarily including those persons on expressly terminal appointments.

5   [Footnote omitted.]

6   [Footnote omitted.]

7   [Footnote omitted.]

8   [Footnote omitted.]

9   [Footnote omitted.]

10   [Footnote omitted.]

"On University Discipline for Disruptive Conduct"

1   The full charge to the committee is set forth as Appendix I [omitted here] to this report.

2   The *Report of the Ad Hoc Committee on Protest and Dissent* and the 2015 *Report of
the Committee on Freedom of Expression* and the *Freedom of Expression Report* are
set forth as Appendix II [omitted here] to this report.

3   We also recommend that the University retain the latitude to make non-substantive revisions to the procedures, from time to time and subject to approval by the Provost, when such are warranted.

4   We recommend that the *Student Manual* include examples of protests that are likely to be regarded as non-disruptive as well as those that are likely to be disruptive. Non-disruptive protests include: marches that do not drown out speakers; silent vigils; protest signs at an event that do not block the vision of the audience; and boycotts of speakers or events. Disruptive protests include: blocking access to an event or to a University facility and shouting or otherwise interrupting an event or other University activity with noise in a way that prevents the event or activity from continuing in its normal course.

Major Works Cited

Bell, Laird. "Are We Afraid of Freedom? A Statement from the Chairman of the Board of Trustees of the University of Chicago." *Bulletin of the American Association of University Professors (1915–1955)* 35, no. 2 (Summer 1949): 301–12. https://doi.org/10.2307/40220354.

Committee of the Council, "A Statement on Academic Freedom." July 12, 1949. Box 2, folder 1. Hutchins Administration Records. Hanna Holborn Gray Special Collections Research Center. University of Chicago Library.

Harper, William Rainey. "Freedom of Speech." In "The Thirty-Sixth Quarterly Statement of the President of the University" (December 18, 1900). *University Record* 5, no. 42 (1901): 375–78. https://campub.lib.uchicago.edu/view/?docId=mvol-0007-0005-0042#page/2/mode/1up.

Hoang, Kimberly Kay. "Aims of Education Address 2021." University of Chicago, September 21, 2021. https://college.uchicago.edu/student-life/aims-education-address-2021-kimberly-kay-hoang.

Hutchins, Robert M. "What Is a University?" April 18, 1935. Box 357, folder 18. Robert Maynard Hutchins Papers. Hanna Holborn Gray Special Collections Research Center. University of Chicago Library.

"Kalven Committee: Report on the University's Role in Political and Social Action." *University of Chicago Record* 1, no. 1 (1967): 2–3. https://campub.lib.uchicago.edu/view/?docId=mvol-0446-0001-0001#page/1/mode/1up.

Lear, Gabriel Richardson. "Aims of Education Address 2018." University
    of Chicago, September 27, 2018. https://college.uchicago.edu
    /student-life/aims-education-address-2018-gabriel-richardson-lear.

Levi, Edward H. "Unrest and the Universities." December 11, 1968.
    Box 298, folder 8, Edward H. Levi Papers. Hanna Holborn Gray Special
    Collections Research Center. University of Chicago Library.

Report of the Ad Hoc Committee on Protest and Dissent. University of
    Chicago, January 13, 2014. https://provost.uchicago.edu/sites/default
    /files/documents/reports/Report%20Protest%20and%20Dissent.pdf.

Report of the Committee on Freedom of Expression. University of Chicago,
    [2015]. https://provost.uchicago.edu/sites/default/files/documents
    /reports/FOECommitteeReport.pdf.

A Report of the University of Chicago Committee on the Criteria
    of Academic Appointment. *University of Chicago Record* 4, no. 6
    (1970): 1–15. https://campub.lib.uchicago.edu/view/?docId=mvol
    -0446-0004-0006#page/1/mode/1up; and *University of Chicago
    Record* 6, no. 1 (1972): 4–6. https://campub.lib.uchicago.edu
    /view/?docId=mvol-0446-0006-0001#page/7/mode/1up.

Revised Final Report of the Committee on University Discipline for
    Disruptive Conduct. University of Chicago, June 2, 2017. https://pro
    vost.uchicago.edu/sites/default/files/DCCRevisedFinal%20%286-2
    -2017%29.pdf.

Stone, Geoffrey R. "Aims of Education Address 2016." University
    of Chicago, September 22, 2016. https://college.uchicago.edu
    /student-life/aims-education-address-2016-geoffrey-r-stone.

Zimmer, Robert J. "Liberal Arts, Free Expression, and the Demosthenes-
    Feynman Trap" (October 20, 2017). American Council of Trustees and
    Alumni, December 13, 2017. https://www.goacta.org/wp-content
    /uploads/ee/download/Liberal-Arts-Free-Expression-and-the
    -Demosthenes-Feynman-Trap.pdf